BEYOND THE LOOKING GLASS

Daily Devotions for Overcoming Anorexia and Bulimia

REMUDA RANCH

THOMAS NELSON PUBLISHERS
Nashville

Published in Nashville, Tennessee, by Thomas Nelson,
Inc., and distributed in Canada by Lawson Falle, Ltd.,
Cambridge, Ontario.

Scripture quotations are from the NEW KING JAMES
VERSION of the Bible. Copyright © 1979, 1980, 1982,
Thomas Nelson, Inc., Publishers.

Scripture quotations noted KJV are from the KING JAMES
VERSION of the Bible. Those noted NAS are from THE
NEW AMERICAN STANDARD BIBLE, Copyright © 1960,
1962, 1963, 1968, 1971, 1972, 1973, 1975, 1977 by
The Lockman Foundation and are used by permission.
Those noted TLB are from *The Living Bible* (Wheaton,
Illinois: Tyndale House Publishers, 1971) and are used by
permission. Those noted RSV are from the REVISED
STANDARD VERSION of the Bible. Copyright © 1946,
1952, 1971, 1973 by the Division of Christian education of
the National Council of the Churches of Christ in the U.S.A.
Used by permission. Those noted NIV are from The Holy
Bible: NEW INTERNATIONAL VERSION. Copyright ©
1978 by the New York International Bible Society. Used by
permission of Zondervan Bible Publishers.

**Library of Congress Cataloging-in-Publication
data can be found in the back of this book.**

Printed in the United States of America
1 2 3 4 5 6 7 — 97 96 95 94 93 92

This book is dedicated to the glory of a faithful God
who gives us "a garment of praise
instead of a spirit of despair."
(Isaiah 61:3 NIV)

Introduction

When our ten-year-old daughter, Jena, stopped eating, my wife, Kay, proceeded to take her to a number of doctors. The professionals were mystified as to the reason for her lack of appetite.

Jena was seen by many doctors without being diagnosed. It was alarming to see her play with her food. She would mash it and shift it around on her plate. She appeared to be eating, but her weight continued to drop.

Finally, we were given a diagnosis: Jena had Anorexia Nervosa; she was starving herself to death. At that point her weight had plummeted from her normal seventy pounds to only forty-eight pounds! The answer seemed simple to me; we just had to make her eat!

As a businessman I was accustomed to my wishes being carried out, but my attempts to help my daughter proved futile.

Over a period of time, God showed us that there was more to Jena's illness than her obsession with food. We have seen a healing take place in our daughter's life, and He has been faithful to us as we continue in our process of recovery.

God used our experience and pain to create Remuda Ranch Center for Anorexia and Bulimia. It is a blessing to be used in the lives of hurting people.

Ward Keller

BRAND NEW

A new time,
A new day,
A new year,
Maybe this time, dear Lord
A new me!

I'll leave behind
The old shell of insecurities,
And travel the road to wholeness.
I'll put my faith in you, Lord,
And learn to love this gift of life
You've given me.

> *Finally, brethren, whatever things are true,*
> *whatever things are noble, whatever things are just,*
> *whatever things are pure, whatever things are*
> *lovely, whatever things are of good report, . . . if*
> *there is anything praiseworthy—meditate on*
> *these things.*
> —Phil. 4:8

It's one of those days! I overslept, and then I spilled coffee on my new suit. Rush-hour traffic was even worse than usual. My kids are whining, and my husband is grumpy. To top it off, I haven't even studied for the chemistry quiz that I'm about to take.

Whatever it is that is upsetting me, I have a choice to make. I can replay every detail in my mind until I am really depressed, or I can take a few deep breaths and try to put things in perspective. I can choose to tell myself, "Okay, I've had some misfortune today. But the sun is shining, and the leaves are turning into a rainbow of colors. I can get through this day."

Do you choose to dwell on the bad things, or do you look for something good to think about? The choice is yours to make!

Father, as I ponder the majesty of a world created for those like me, I wonder why it is that I can't just let God set me free. Please hear my prayer, oh Lord, I pray, my crying heart, hurt and dismay, my pride, my fears, I'll throw away. For your healing grace, dear Lord, I pray. The mountains bold, the oceans blue, the sunrise bright, the stars, the moon, this earth I love, you gave to me. I think I'll let you set me free.

But You, O LORD, are a shield for me,
My glory and the One who lifts up my head.
—Ps. 3:3

Today I am going to remember to put on the shield of my Lord. When my kids quarrel, he will protect me from feeling discouraged. When my husband criticizes me, I will rely on God's strength to keep me from falling prey to my husband's opinions of me.

God's shield will protect me from acting out of frustration when I see the dogs in the trash again. When life takes the usual dips and turns I will remind myself that God can lift up my head when I am feeling blue.

Unless I recall the shield of God, I am likely to fall into the trap of self-pity and depression. When I feel bowed with the worries of my day, God is able to lift me up and give me strength.

Today, I'll hold up my head and say, "I'm O.K.! God is my shield and my strength; I can face what this day will bring." Life's trials cannot do me in with the power of God that I receive through Jesus Christ.

Life's little irritations, as well as the huge obstacles in my life, are no match for my God.

———

Abba, Father, help me to remember that you are my shield against all of life's trials.

*When I kept silent about my sin, my body wasted away
Through my groaning all day long.*   —Ps. 32:3 NAS

Silence was the core of my eating disorder. I became uncommunicative about what I really felt with my family, friends, and, most of all, God.

This silence put me in a lonely world where intimacy was only a dream and shame controlled my life. The more withdrawn I became on the outside, the louder the groaning became on the inside. I punished my body to silence the pain, and the wasting away began.

This cycle continued until I became willing to break the silence and walk through the painful process of healing. Breaking the silence with God and those I love was the first step I took toward wholeness.

My progress in recovery has been marked by my ability to remain honest and open about things that are easily left unsaid.

Father, help me risk sharing openly and honestly with you and others so the guilt of my sin does not leave me in shame.

*Come to Me, all you who labor and are heavy
laden, and I will give you rest.* —Matt. 11:28

At times I do not even recognize the burdens I am
bearing. I can function quite adequately for some time
under steady pressure. The emotional pain motivates
me to keep moving; if I stop, I might have to deal with
the pain. Instead, I keep going, hardly aware of the
underlying current of stress in my life.

Physically the stress is acted out in much the same
way. For weeks I live with minor headaches, and I do
not even grant them validity with a pain reliever. I become accustomed to the dull pain in my head until I
hardly notice it. I stay so busy that I do not even allow
myself time to sit and rest. That might be all I need,
just some quiet time to rest myself, collect my
thoughts, and gather my strength to continue.

Recently my headaches increased to such a degree
that I was forced to stop and rest. My sight started
to blur. I lost my peripheral vision, and then it happened—I got a full-blown migraine headache.

My emotional pain cannot go unchecked forever.
The dull ache in my heart keeps increasing. The only
way I know to deal with that is to ask God for the
strength to look at where the pain is coming from and
to allow him to walk me through it.

Father, I release my burdens to you.

What a man desires is unfailing love.
—Prov. 19:22 NIV

I am a great caretaker! In my attempts to gain love and acceptance, there is no end to what I will do for others. But where do I go to be cared for?

As a mom and wife, most of my energy is directed toward the needs of others. Without thinking, I can feed and dress the children, plan meals for the family, and start on the to-do list that never ends.

But it is with much effort that I meet even the most basic of my needs. This comes from an overwhelming sense of unworthiness and shame. The events of my past have convinced me that I do not deserve the things that I would gladly give to others.

I see no hope of ever believing I'm of value unless I learn to be cared for by God. I long to believe that I am truly loved and accepted by him.

In my hurry to care for others, there seems to be no time for me! It helps when I realize that God is able to care for me in a way that no one else can.

Father, remind me that your love for me is complete.

My little children, these things I write to you, so
that you may not sin. And if anyone sins, we have
an Advocate with the Father, Jesus Christ the
righteous.
—1 John 2:1

As a Christian I want to make good use of the talents God has given me. Before recovery I was rarely satisfied with my performance because it was always short of perfection.

Now I have a new outlook on life. Where I used to strive for perfection, now I aim for excellence. This is a standard that is both challenging and attainable. I have found myself becoming more confident and content.

I understand that God does not want me to waste the abilities he has given me. However, he knows I will not reach all of my goals because of my humanness. I will sometimes miss the mark or sin.

Thankfully, Jesus Christ sacrificed his life for these sins. Because of this unmerited gift and the grace of God, I don't have to be perfect to inherit eternal life. Praise God, from whom all blessings flow.

Father, again I thank you for releasing me from the prison of perfection.

Hear me when I call, O God of my righteousness!
You have relieved me in my distress;
Have mercy on me, and hear my prayer.

—Ps. 4:1

While I was practicing my eating disorder I never felt much of anything. If I was in danger of feeling emotions, a quick trip to the refrigerator provided a numbing agent. If life seemed out of control, I gained a sense of control by restricting my intake of food.

Since I learned other ways to deal with life, I have experienced a whole new range of emotions. It is frightening to experience life for the first time at age twenty-eight! Things that most people take for granted are new and different to me.

At times my feelings threaten to overwhelm me. The pain of horrible memories seems more than I can bear. Sometimes I am afraid I can't stand the intense emotional stress for even another second. During those times journaling helps me. I can look back and see that I felt distressed before and lived through it.

I am thankful to say that God has been with me in my times of pain. He has brought relief when life seemed unmanageable. It is because of God that I am still alive today! I can continue on through the pain because I know that God will be by my side.

Lord, please relieve my distress!

> *These things I have spoken to you, that in Me*
> *you may have peace. In the world you will have*
> *tribulation; but be of good cheer, I have overcome*
> *the world.*
> —John 16:33

I am such a sucker! I was told a lie somewhere along the way, and I grabbed it hook, line, and sinker. I thought if only I did what was right, life would be smooth sailing. Was I ever wrong!

In John 16:33 it says "you will have tribulation." Why did I think it would be different? It does not say I might have a few problems or a little bump in life. I am going to have trouble! I can't change that fact.

What I can change is my reaction to life's pain. I have stopped telling myself, "I'm doing something wrong if I feel pain." I no longer believe that life should be pain-free. That helps a little bit.

Another change I've made is not trying to get out of the pain as fast as I can. I've learned that God uses pain to teach me.

I have also stopped pretending that I'm not bothered by tribulation. I always tried to ignore it or at least not let it get me down. The reality of life is that tribulation hurts; my heart aches! I've found that people aren't shocked when I tell them I'm hurting. Some are even able to give encouragement.

Lord, help me learn through the pain.

> *You will keep him in perfect peace,*
> *Whose mind is stayed on You,*
> *Because he trusts in You.*
> —Isa. 26:3

At times I get caught up in the worries of the day; so many things require my attention. Often my mind is so consumed with my worries that I am not able to function! I become emotionally paralyzed.

It's easy to become so focused on the issues at hand that I lose sight of God. I have no peace at all! My only thought is to get free of the pain.

As if real worries are not enough, when I am at my lowest point I begin to focus on my body. In order to distract myself from reality, I choose to obsess about my looks.

Dwelling on my weight or the fact that my stomach is not flat does not bring any peace. It only serves to heighten my anxiety. The only possible way to gain peace when everything is out of control is by looking to God.

Yes, I have marriage problems, but I am loved by God. Finances are a big pressure, but God continues to provide peace. My friends seem to be so distant right now, but my heavenly Father will not forsake me! Life seems so hectic and unpredictable, but God is constant and stable and always there for me.

Lord, thank you for the peace that comes when I turn my thoughts toward you.

Though he stumble, he will not fall,
For the LORD upholds him with his hand.
—Ps. 37:24 NIV

I've not only stumbled, I've fallen hard. Recovery is hard work, and I frequently find myself doing the same old unhealthy stuff. It usually happens so fast that I forget to reach out for the Lord's hand.

I believe God's Word is absolutely true. God says that I will not fall, that he won't let me. He sees things differently than I do. I'm so hard on myself that I see every slip or stumble as a failure, but God doesn't see it that way. I am encouraged to know that I'm doing better than I thought I was.

When I get to heaven, God will say to me, "You did a great job! I'm proud of you." I can bask in that praise now. I can hold my head up and continue to work my recovery knowing that every little stumble isn't a disaster.

I haven't fallen, I'm just momentarily off balance. I can move with confidence. I can recover!

God, you give me the confidence to know that I will not fall.

> *The fear of man brings a snare,*
> *But whoever trusts in the LORD shall be safe.*
> —Prov. 29:25

For eight years, I have lived in the metropolis of Phoenix, Arizona. It is a huge city with lots to see, but my fears have prevented me from experiencing all that is available.

Because I was so obsessed with myself, it was impossible to venture out of my regular routine. I had very limited contact with a few people, and my activities were monotonous and predictable. I escaped into food to numb myself and to keep from being involved with life.

In the year since I got treatment for my eating disorder, I have been free to do much more than I ever thought possible! My little world used to consist of a few square miles; now I have the courage to venture out into new areas.

I realize that my fears had paralyzed me to such an extent that my view of life was growing smaller all the time. I did not expect anything from life because I was unwilling to step out of my "comfort zone."

I feel empowered when I am able to break through the fears that ruled my life for so many years. It is frightening sometimes, but the joy of experiencing life far outweighs the pain of the fear.

I am learning to trust the Lord with my fears. He helps me push myself when I feel like staying stuck in safe, dull routines.

Lord, give me the courage to push through the fears.

My eyes are ever toward the LORD,
For He shall pluck my feet out of the net.
—Ps. 25:15

I have tried many ways to get over my eating disorder. Many times I have said to myself, "I promise I'll eat tomorrow" or "This is the last time I'm going to binge." My intentions were good, but they failed me.

The desire to get well is only part of the process. I must also rely on God's strength to do for me what I am unable to do for myself. That is hard, because I have told myself that I have to be in control. What a trap!

The only way I have been able to break destructive habits is by learning to give up control to God, who is more than able to win this battle! As I keep my eyes on God and ask for his help, I become less and less tangled up in this net of disordered eating. It is such a relief!

Lord, help me to keep my eyes on you. Please release me from this disease.

> *And do not be conformed to this world, but be*
> *transformed by the renewing of your mind.*
>
> —Rom. 12:2

When I look at those skinny little models in the magazines, with their gaunt faces and staring eyes, I wonder what price they pay for their "ideal" bodies. Do their hearts hold the hurts of a lifetime? I shake my head and say, "There, but for the grace of God, go I!"

It is so easy to listen to the lies of this world. The false gods whisper in my ear, "Thin is happy; thin is beautiful; thin is smart; thin is successful; thin is . . ." until I almost believe them.

I am constantly being bombarded with subtle and not-so-subtle messages about the way I "should" look, dress, act, talk, and live. The world's standards for me are not necessarily what God wants.

This world tells me that my entire worth is based on external things, that how I look is more important than who I am. One of the gods of this world is money, so if I don't have enough, then I am told that I am worthless. I am told to dress a certain way, even if that style is not the most attractive for my shape. Am I not more valuable than the brand of shoes I buy?

When I look at the false idols in the catalogs, I try to remember that God loves me just the way I am. He accepts my body, lumps, bumps, and sags. I am beautiful in the eyes of the Lord.

Dear Lord, help me see the real beauty in me.

*And you shall know the truth, and the truth shall
make you free.*
       —John 8:32

My whole life had been built on secrets, deception,
and lies. I hid my thoughts and feelings as well as the
fact that I was being controlled by an eating disorder.
Truth and freedom were not words that fit my life.

I've often thought about how much energy I've
wasted concealing binges or rearranging the food on
my plate to make it look as though I had eaten when I
had not. I had so much shame bottled up inside me
over all my deceptive ways.

The only sure-fire way I know to release all the destructive power of the shame is to tell the truth! It is
painful to come clean with people to whom we've lied,
but it is worth it to be free of shame.

I ask God daily to give me the strength to be honest
so that I can keep from being buried under that terrible
pile of shame. It works for me, and I know he will give
you the courage to be honest if you only ask!

*Dear Father, please help me be truthful, and let that truth set me free
as you have promised.*

> *A voice was heard in Ramah,*
> *Lamentation, weeping, and great mourning,*
> *Rachel weeping for her children,*
> *Refusing to be comforted,*
> *Because they are no more.*   —Matt. 2:18

In this verse Matthew refers to the fulfillment of a prophecy by Jeremiah. Jeremiah predicted the killing of all boys in Bethlehem under the age of two. It was ordered by King Herod after the birth of Christ.

This verse might have been written for twentieth-century women like this:

> A voice is heard in America, weeping and great mourning, women who have had abortions weeping for their children, and refusing to be comforted, because they are no more.

Losing a child to death is one of life's great tragedies. Many families cannot survive it; the divorce rate is alarming among families who lose children.

Having endured the tragedy of abortion, I can say that this is one of my greatest losses. The loss of my little one is a pain that has taken much time to grieve. The guilt and shame I feel over this incident has caused me to want to die. I have tried to punish my body to relieve me from the guilt.

Numbing myself with food has not taken away the shame. I have found peace through admitting my sin to God and accepting his forgiveness.

Father, remind me that I am clean in your eyes.

Whenever I am afraid,
I will trust in You.
In God (I will praise His word),
In God I have put my trust;
I will not fear.
What can flesh do to me?
                    —Ps. 56:3–4

Since my trust was violated, I now view life through a cloud of suspicion and doubt. I often feel incapable of truly trusting God, others, and even my own instincts. I live in constant fear of being hurt again.

A therapist once told me, "Give up on trusting, just surrender!" That concept helped so much. In my mind, trust means struggling and straining to hold on to God for survival. I have a different idea of surrender; I see it as a lack of effort, just being able to let go completely.

My fears—of relapse, of rejection, and of failure—all stem from my lack of ability to trust God. As long as I pretend to be in control I have no hope of overcoming this eating disorder.

Part of the cure is to learn that God is worthy of my trust. No matter how fearful I am, I know that his arms are strong enough to catch me safely!

God, teach me to trust you, but until I am able to do that, help me to keep surrendering.

> *Then Jesus said to the centurion, "Go your way;*
> *and as you have believed, so let it be done for you."*
> *And his servant was healed that same hour.*
> —Matt. 8:13

This centurion did not profess to be a follower of Christ, but his faith was great. He asked for his servant to be healed, and he believed that it would be accomplished if Christ would only speak the words.

When I entered treatment, my heart had been wounded by those who called themselves Christians. It was hard for me to separate what I had been taught as a child from the real truth of the Bible. Other women had the same difficulty. Each had to come to God through her own unique perspective.

Through my prayer journal, I see God's faithfulness. I have kept the prayer requests from friends in recovery; each tattered sheet is filled with memories of special women. Today, as I look back, I see how God has answered many of the requests that were lifted up to him in prayer. My faith is strengthened, and I continue to trust God with my requests.

Father, I thank you for your faithfulness.

For my iniquities have gone over my head;
Like a heavy burden they are too heavy for me. . . .
I am feeble and severely broken;
I groan because of the turmoil of my heart. . . .
For in You, O LORD, I hope;
You will hear, O Lord my God.   —Ps. 38:4, 8, 15

These verses are my cry as I am caught in the ravages of an eating disorder. Though I wrestle with the things in my past that have contributed to my present state, I also know that my own mismanagement has added to the chaos.

What makes these first steps of recovery so very difficult? I believe it is because they strike at the very heart of my deepest human flaws. Even in the throes of an eating disorder, I believe that I really should be able to control all events that have anything to do with my life. Lucifer, the right-hand angel of God, demonstrated this same arrogance when he decided that he could rule the universe as well as God! So I cling to my powerlessness to guard me from that destructive arrogance.

My heart is also full of insecurity and fear because I know I am flawed. I scramble to assure others that I am worthy in an attempt to hide my shame. I know that God is my only hope in ending this internal war.

Lord, remind me that you know my struggles and that I'm acceptable to you in any state.

> *I press toward the goal for the prize of the upward*
> *call of God in Christ Jesus.* —Phil. 3:14

One year out of treatment and I'm still not fixed! There is still pain in my life and all my problems are not gone! Today I feel like giving up.

I must remember what I gained from my time in treatment. I have eleven months of abstinence from disordered eating, I am working on changing the ugly thought patterns that have always been a part of me, and I am more confident than I have ever been in my life.

I never believed that I was adequate to do anything before. I went from living at my dad's house to living with my husband. I never was just me, and I did not feel capable of doing anything on my own.

Right now I am on my own, and it's scary! But I am capable; I can do things without being dependent on someone else. The things I learned in treatment prepared me for life. I learned more than just how to let go of my eating disorder.

I feel discouraged right now because everything is not perfect, but God has brought me this far, so I won't quit now. I will press on with his help; the prize is yet to come.

Father, give me the strength to go on when I feel like quitting.

Then God saw everything that He had made, and indeed it was very good.
—Gen. 1:31

When I was bulimic, I looked into the mirror and hated what I saw. Yet when I looked at the stars, the mountains, the sunset, I would praise God for what he had made. I was unable to praise him for making me. In fact, I resented him for making me the way he had.

Accepting the truth that God created me was hard. To be honest, it still is at times. But it is a brick wall that I must break through in order to continue in recovery.

I look in the mirror and ask myself, "Did God make everything perfect but me? Did he use leftovers to make me?" The Bible says, "I am fearfully and wonderfully made" (Ps. 139:14). "Then God saw everything that He had made, and indeed it was very good" (Gen. 1:31a).

He created each of us fearfully and wonderfully, not some better than others. The perfect body we strive for, even kill ourselves for, is a human ideal, not God's. God truly does not make junk!

Father, help me see myself today as someone you created with loving hands.

> *Your word is a lamp to my feet*
> *And a light to my path.*
> —Ps. 119:105

At times I think I have really been enlightened; I know so much more now than I ever have! When I entered treatment I knew very little about the roots of my eating disorder. After nine weeks I probably could have written a book with all that I had learned!

So why are things still unclear? I thought I knew what to do! I am pleased with the lack of control food has over me, but other issues are not so easy to fix. Most of my problems left the treatment center right along with me.

Usually I am able to think through things fairly well, but right now everything seems muddled. I am having trouble finding the answers; I feel like I'm stumbling around in the dark.

I have stopped looking to God for my answers, and that's why I'm in this mess. I can't decide whose advice to take: My therapist has her ideas, my husband has made his views clear, and my friends are making their feelings very evident.

Maybe none of those answers is right for me! I have found that God makes his voice clear to me if I take the time to listen to him. Sometimes he speaks through people, and other times he directs me through his Word. He sheds light on those areas where I am in the dark.

Lord, help me to see your light.

There is a way that seems right to a man,
But its end is the way of death.
—Prov. 14:12

At first my eating disorder just seemed to come naturally. It did not occur to me that I was using food to cover my shame and hide my feelings. But as it progressed, the disease seemed to take on a life of its own. With a personality resembling an angry teenager, it protected the scared, sad child inside me.

That eating disorder became a source of both relief and torment for me. Although I drew incredible strength from it, I was completely powerless to overcome it. My drive to be in control became an intense obsession.

At one point I thought I had achieved ultimate control, but it all came crashing down around me. Sitting in a hospital bed, with a tube forcing the dreaded calories into my body, I felt utterly helpless. I saw the distortions in my thinking. Rather than being in control, I had lost control!

Acknowledging my condition was the first step toward change. Recovery began when I surrendered to God.

Father, help me continue to follow your way.

God is faithful.
—1 Cor. 1:9

It is so easy to fall into the trap of depending on people. I want people to fill me up and make the pain stop! My needs consume me to such a degree that I latch on to those around me to keep myself from falling.

The problem with depending on people is that they are not always dependable! My husband sometimes responds to me in ways that hurt me. My therapist is not always there when I need her. Friends are busy dealing with their own lives. So what are my options for getting my needs met?

Part of becoming healthy is learning to turn to God with my needs. He is never too busy to listen to me and hear me cry. God doesn't take lunch breaks. He will always make time for me.

In my loneliness I still reach out for a human touch to reassure me; God designed me with those needs. But when the people around are not able to mend my aching heart, the only solution is to turn to God.

Sometimes it is hard for me to feel God's presence. I have to remind myself that my feelings are not always reliable. God's Word tells me that he is faithful. I choose to believe that.

Lord, please help me rely on you to fill my needs. Teach me not to look to people to do your job.

But the goat on which the lot fell to be the scapegoat shall be presented alive before the LORD, to make atonement upon it, and to let it go as the scapegoat into the wilderness. —Lev. 16:10

An amazing thing has taken place since I got treatment for my eating disorder. I am now the official, designated sick one of the family. Since I have a diagnosed problem and I admitted that I could not get over it without help, many of my family members now view me as the cause of their problems.

This is a great relief to my loved ones, since they no longer have to face their own issues. Everything can be channeled through me now. History is being rewritten with me as the villain in every era.

I will not sit and stew about the unfairness of it all. Knowing this does challenge me to look inside, though. I want to honestly admit my shortcomings and change those areas of my life with God's help. I am learning to take responsibility for things that are my fault, and not accept guilt for others' flaws.

Lord, help me not to act out the role of scapegoat, even when I have been cast in that light.

You have turned for me my mourning into dancing.
—Ps. 30:11

In the strict home where I grew up, I was not allowed to dance. Dancing was seen as unacceptable behavior for a young girl in my church.

After I developed an eating disorder, I became more and more inhibited about my body. I hated every part of it; nothing seemed acceptable or attractive. I envied people who were comfortable with themselves. I longed to feel confident like others seemed to be.

I began to feel stiff and ill-at-ease in my movements, and I tried hard to control my every move. The result was that I appeared tense and uptight. Even when I thought I was relaxed, my movements were rigid.

I entered treatment for my eating disorder in November of 1990. I spent Thanksgiving, Christmas, and New Year's in the treatment center.

On New Year's Eve we all celebrated together and really let off steam. I'll never forget that night because it was the first time I had ever danced! In sweats and jammies, we looked pretty silly, but the love and acceptance there made it a safe place to let loose!

Father, set me free in my body, soul, and spirit!

To everything there is a season,
A time for every purpose under heaven
                              —Ecol. 3:1

Many times since leaving the safety of the treatment center, I have longed to go back. There were days when I felt I could not make it in the real world. Even though the things I dealt with in treatment were excruciatingly painful, it was a safe, womb-like environment. I felt love and acceptance like never before.

I know I can never go back in time. That place with the special set of people and circumstances can never be recreated. But I am thankful for that opportunity to make changes in my life.

I don't miss the buildings or the geographic location. I long for the feelings of safety and security that I experienced there. God used people to create that season of healing for me.

There is a special spot in my heart where those memories remain. I can revisit that place in my heart when the pain of life threatens to overwhelm me.

———————

Thank you, Father, for creating my mind with the ability to remember the seasons of life.

And they were all amazed at the majesty of God.
—Luke 9:43

I struggle to see God as he really is. In my own human-ness, I am likely to view him as I do other authority figures in my life. It is hard to trust God when I picture him in human terms.

Many of the people in authority in my life did not use their power wisely. My father had a problem keeping his anger in check. I remember teachers who ruled with an iron hand. Several men in my life used my body for their own purposes.

I still tend to see God through the eyes of a fright-ened little child. Trust does not come easily for some-one who has been violated.

It is easy to turn to food out of fear. I often ate to feel secure; food was always there and never let me down. I thought food was something that I could control—that is, until it controlled me.

That I have been abstinent since entering treatment almost one year ago is a tribute to God's power in my life! There is simply no other explanation for it. He has used that miracle to prove himself to me and many others who suffer with eating disorders.

Father, keep reminding me that you are not susceptible to human weakness.

The Lord is close to the brokenhearted,
and saves those who are crushed in spirit.
—Ps. 34:18 NIV

My recovery was a long and often painful process. As I opened up old wounds, my heart was broken all over again.

My spirit was crushed as I admitted the hurts I had dealt to those I loved the most. When I looked at all the lying and manipulating I had done in the midst of my bulimia, my heart ached so deeply I thought it would never stop.

I pleaded with God to take the pain away. I found that I was no longer able to bury my wounds under mounds of food. This time I was powerless to stop the pain, and I cried out to God.

God's answer was not to relieve me of the pain. I needed to hurt so I could realize the depth of my self-destructiveness. But God was with me in all my pain. He answered my cry for help by showing me his promise to be with me. He held me up and kept me going when I was crushed in spirit. When I didn't think I could go on his presence was near me, and that saved me.

How wonderful it is to realize that he knows my pain and keeps me close to him.

Thank you, dear Father, for keeping me close and for holding me up.

> *So I have come down to deliver them out of the*
> *hand of the Egyptians, and to bring them up from*
> *that land to a good and large land, to a land*
> *flowing with milk and honey.* —Ex. 3:8

I have been to the land flowing with milk and honey; it is my grandmother's house in Arkansas. There is food everywhere you look, and huge meals seem to appear around the clock! My grandmother's way of showing love is through her cooking; she gives love by filling you full of food.

Not only are the meals huge, but the candy jar is always full. Little dishes of candy are placed strategically in every room. Eating is a constant focus; one meal is barely finished when the discussion of what to eat next begins.

A short visit to my grandmother's house can be nice, but staying for long can be hazardous to your health.

I have worked hard to separate my emotions from my eating. I do not want food to equal love and security. I want my life to be full, but not full of food. I want to fill myself with other worthy things.

Lord, teach me to dream of a land filled with love, peace, security, and contentment.

He lifted me out of the slimy pit,
out of the mud and mire;
He set my feet on a rock
and gave me a firm place to stand.
He put a new song in my mouth. . . .
I said, "O LORD, have mercy on me."
—Ps. 40:2–3a; 41:4a NIV

Driving along in my car one day, I was feeling very discouraged about my life. I was disappointed in the progress I was making in recovery from a twenty-year-old eating disorder. After all, I had been in two treatment centers, spent hours in counseling, and had heard lots of teaching from God's Word. I desire to live a life pleasing to God. Shouldn't my life be falling into place by now? I was in the grips of depression and anger. I felt defeated.

Then a beautiful song came on the radio. The words were close to the words of Psalms 40 and 41. "Oh Lord, have mercy on me and heal me! Place my feet upon a rock! Put a new song in my heart. Oh Lord, have mercy on me." The words and music flowed over me like a soothing oil. It was as if God were saying, "You try so hard; you work so hard! Let me put your feet on the rock and put the song in your heart. Let me heal you!"

———————

Thank you, Lord, for having mercy on me. Please heal me!

Odd
this twisted form
should be
the work of
God.
God
Who makes,
without mistakes,
the happy norm,
the status quo,
the usual,
made me,
you know.
The Royal Palm
He made;
and, too,
the stunted pine.
With joy
I see the lovely shapes.
With pride
I live in mine.

No accident I am;
a Master Craftsman's plan.

> *So when Jesus had received the sour wine, He said,*
> *"It is finished!" And bowing His head, He gave up*
> *His spirit.*
> —John 19:30

I am so grateful that Jesus gave his all so I can be free from my sins! At any point in the process he might have given up and quit before the task was completed. I'm convinced that he did not want to die. Christ's words in Matthew 26:39 reveal that he was definitely open to a different plan if it was made available to him.

A lesser man might have given up as he was dragging the heavy cross to the hill. The pain of carrying that burden on a back that had been lacerated and shredded would have been enough to cause many to lie down and die.

If my friends denied they even knew me in my greatest time of need, I'm afraid I would decide that the cost was too great for me to pay. Jesus Christ went the whole nine yards. He did not quit, even in the face of extreme pain.

I have been given a task: My job is to recover from the eating disorders of anorexia, bulimia, and compulsive overeating. This task seems too big for me, but I am not expected to do it alone. God is with me, and he has provided support in the form of groups, therapists, and friends. I choose not to quit! I will continue to recover with God's help!

Lord Jesus, thank you for your example to me.

My heart is severely pained within me,
And the terrors of death have fallen upon me.
Fearfulness and trembling have come upon
me,
And horror has overwhelmed me.
—Ps. 55:4–5

My memories of the months before I entered treatment for my eating disorder seem like a nightmare now. I was completely out of control with food; I was in a dazed state from bingeing and purging up to twenty times each day.

At first I did not see how I could take time out of life to get help for my disease. Then I realized that if I did not take the time my life would soon be over.

Admitting that I had an eating disorder and was suicidal was painful. I had always prided myself on being able to do anything, and now I was faced with something I could not handle.

Because I had been so secretive for thirteen years, it was hard to convince my husband and family that I was in danger. The news of my disease came as quite a shock to people.

I kept putting off entering treatment. There were days when the denial was so strong, I actually thought I could get better on my own! Even as I write, it is hard for me to believe that I really took nine weeks out of my life to address the pain inside me. I am so thankful that God preserved my life until I was willing to do my part and seek help!

Thank you, Father, for the chance at a new life!

> *For the LORD does not see as man sees; for man looks at the outward appearance, but the LORD looks at the heart.*
> —1 Sam. 16:7

My body is not perfect. It is not now and never will be without the bumps and bulges that annoy me. Some of my body parts remind me of people I'd rather not be like. But guess what? It's my body.

I'm working on accepting myself right now, the way I am. I can't wait to accept myself until after I've lost another ten pounds, or after I've firmed up those flabby spots. This is not an excuse to become lazy and unhealthy. I just need to feel okay and love myself in this state of imperfection.

I'm not perfect on the inside either. There are some pretty ugly spots in the corners of my heart. My thoughts are unhealthy at times as well. My words cause pain in others more often than I care to admit.

I don't want to be guilty of working only on the imperfections that are visible to others. I want to become the person God wants me to be, inside and out.

God, help me to remember that you love me even though I'm not perfect.

He went a little farther and fell on His face, and prayed, saying, "O My Father, if it is possible, let this cup pass from Me; nevertheless, not as I will, but as You will."

—Matt. 26:39

Believe me, I am open to any new ideas on how to recover from my eating disorder. I'm at the place where I keep falling on my face begging God to take the pain away. I've tried bargaining with him: "I'll do anything if you fix me right now!"

I struggle desperately with yielding to his will. I seem constantly to be trying to get out of this mess instead of working through it. I want to find a route that is painless, but so far I have not found that way.

I no longer struggle with food daily. That piece of the puzzle has really come together for me. I'm grateful for that; it means that I can focus my attention on the real issues at hand. Once I got my head out of the toilet, I got a good look at the reasons I was there in the first place!

I'm working on becoming willing. It is a matter of an attitude adjustment. Instead of fighting and scratching to get out of the mess I'm in, I want to learn what God can do right in the middle of it all.

Lord, please help me to have a willing heart.

> *He restores my soul;*
> *He leads me in the paths of righteousness*
> *For His name's sake.*
> —Ps. 23:3

I sat alone in the dark one evening feeling hopeless and depressed. Recovery seemed far beyond my grasp and I wondered if it was even worth it to keep trying. What exactly was I trying to accomplish anyway, and how would I know when I had done it?

In the stillness, God spoke the word "restoration" to my heart. He showed me that while I do have to take part in my recovery, the restoration is his job. My part is to utilize every available resource to break the addictive behaviors of my eating disorder. God will bring me beyond recovery and make me whole.

Restoration means bringing back into health and vigor. God's Word tells me that after I've suffered a while, he will perfect, establish, strengthen, and settle me (1 Peter 5:10b).

I have heard it said that "responsibility is our response to God's ability." He has the ability to restore me completely; my response is to make him my partner in recovery.

_____

Father, thank you for the promise to restore me. Help me hold on to that hope.

I am set apart with the dead,
like the slain who lie in the grave,
whom you remember no more,
who are cut off from your care. . . .
You have taken my companions
  and loved ones from me;
the darkness is my closest friend.
  —Ps. 88:5, 18 NIV

Have you ever felt like you were trapped in the dark and no one cared? Even as I recovered from bulimia, depression dogged me. Life was colorless. There was no light at the end of the long tunnel in front of me. Saddest of all, I could not feel God's presence.

I clung to all of Psalm 88, taking some comfort in knowing that if I felt like the psalmist did, God must certainly understand. He does!

Depression clouds thinking and dulls feelings. I couldn't feel God's presence, but he was there. He has been faithful to see me through the darkness. God has promised that he will not leave me or forsake me (Josh. 1:5b). When I feel alone, I hold on to this promise, and I know he understands.

Thank you, Father, for staying with me.

> *For I am persuaded that neither death nor life, nor*
> *angels nor principalities nor powers, nor things*
> *present nor things to come, nor height nor depth,*
> *nor any other created thing, shall be able to*
> *separate us from the love of God which is in*
> *Christ Jesus our Lord.*   —Rom. 8:38–39

I spent most of my life feeling alienated from God. I could not get past my own guilt and shame to believe that God loved me. I was so full of self-hatred that I would not accept the fact that I was worthy of love.

There are still times when I struggle to accept God's forgiveness and his love. When I start dwelling on the things that I have done wrong and the ways I have been wronged by others, God's love seems unattainable. It's a lie that I must somehow earn God's favor; that lie could destroy me if I choose to let it. Instead, I practice telling myself the truth.

The truth is that even though I was molested, raped, and incested as a child, God's love is still accessible to me. Those men who hurt me cannot keep me away from God. Although I grew up in a home where God was not viewed as loving, my parents' ideas of God cannot prevent me from being loved by him. My eating disorder and all the lies and deceit that go along with it cannot separate me from God's love.

Nothing can isolate me from God's love.

Lord, surround me with your love.

*Then He said to them, "My soul is exceedingly
sorrowful, even to death. Stay here and watch
with me."*
                                    —Matt. 26:38

One of the most useful tools I learned in treatment
was how to make my needs known. In the home where
I grew up it was not safe to express needs. My family
played verbal games, and we were caustic and sarcas-
tic with one another.

I made every attempt to eliminate my needs entirely. When that could not be accomplished, I went
without getting many needs met. I feared rejection so
much that I believed it was better to do without than to
express my needs.

I spent my entire life trying to live without any help.
I felt like a failure if I could not accomplish a task without asking for help. I believed I was stupid if I did not
know the answer to all of life's questions.

In this passage of Scripture Jesus Christ admitted his
need for companionship. He was hurting badly and
had asked his friends to stay with him in his time of
trouble. But at the time he needed them most, Jesus'
closest friends failed him.

I have learned to make my needs known, and now I
am learning to live with the disappointment I feel
when my needs go unmet.

Father, give me the courage to express my needs.

When you lie down, you will not be afraid;
Yes, you will lie down and your sleep will be sweet.

—Prov. 3:24

At night when things are quiet and still, my brain goes a million miles an hour. It is hard to turn my mind off when it is time to go to sleep. Often after I finally do go to sleep my night is not restful.

As far as I can tell, my life has not improved greatly for all my nocturnal worrying. Tossing and turning do not change anything, but sleepless nights do have an adverse effect on me.

Life is tough enough even with a full night's sleep. Matters are made more difficult when I am tired and irritable. My stomach seems upset after a night of trying to solve all my problems, and that makes eating right even more of a problem.

In the verses before this passage in Proverbs, I read that I will find peace by keeping God's commands (v. 2). I am told that God will direct my paths if I look to him (v. 6). As I learn to respect God and his wisdom, I will become healthier (v. 8). I am promised happiness and understanding through wisdom (v. 13).

Since my way of working through problems instead of sleeping has not been productive, I choose to follow God's prescription for peace!

Father, may I learn the meaning of true rest as I give my worries to you.

The way of a fool is right in his own eyes,
But he who heeds counsel is wise.
—Prov. 12:15

My own plans have not worked out well. In my attempts to cure my problems with food I've tried every imaginable remedy. Looking back, many of those things seem very foolish.

There were the freeze-dried foods, just like the astronauts took to the moon! For a while, I monitored carbohydrates, and then refrained from sugar and refined starches. Protein drinks hit the market and I looked for a quick fix with them. I took diet pills, fiber pills, and pills to burn fat while I slept! I even went to a faith healer to avoid going into treatment. Each new gimmick seemed right at the time.

I failed to accept that my inability to control my eating was just a symptom of much deeper pain inside me. All those obsessive ways of dealing with food and weight were just ways of running from pain that would eventually have to be faced.

At this point I am trying to be wise and listen to the advice of those God has chosen to be part of my healing. Honestly, I spent a lot more time and energy hiding from the pain than it took to face it head-on and deal with it.

God, may I stop trying to bury my pain with foolish plans and learn to listen to you.

> *Have you found honey?*
> *Eat only as much as you need,*
> *Lest you be filled with it and vomit.*
> —Prov. 25:16

On one of my first outings from the treatment center, I went to dinner with a group of staff and residents from Remuda Ranch. I was terrified! I had become accustomed to eating in front of the women I was in treatment with, but I had not yet made many choices about my food.

I was faced with the fear of eating in front of strangers, even my therapist! On top of that I had to make a choice from an extensive menu. Thankfully, I was sitting close to a woman I had grown to trust who was also in treatment for her eating disorder. I told her how fearful I was and she promised to support me through the meal.

I gasped when my meal arrived; it looked enormous to me! When my therapist saw my face she said, "You don't have to eat it all." That simple statement helped change my life. The thought never occurred to me; I always ate all my food. Sometimes I would even help finish my children's plates. Then, feeling stuffed and guilty, I would throw it all up and start the cycle again.

Since I left treatment, I have been amazed to learn that I can enjoy food without stuffing myself. Now I feel free to leave food on my plate.

Lord, thank you for giving me the chance to learn how much is enough when it comes to food.

Before I was afflicted, I went astray,
But now I keep Your word. . . .
It is good for me that I have been afflicted,
That I may learn Your statutes.
The law of Your mouth is better to me
Than thousands of coins of gold and silver.
—Ps. 119:67, 71–72

I have to admit that when I entered treatment for ano-rexia, I did it for my family. I really did not want to get well. Things were comfortable for me and I certainly did not want to gain weight.

I made a deal with God. I was willing to seek help for my eating disorder if he would restore my relationship with him. And that he did! Through his Word, God filled me with the desire to live.

God used a seemingly impossible situation to bring about good things in my life. Being one thousand miles away from home and family was very painful. But without the responsibilities of being a wife and a mom, I was able to spend time with God and begin to break the hold that anorexia had on me.

I began to thank God for the eating disorder that had control of my life. I was not grateful for the disease itself, but the changes in my life that had happened as a result of dealing with it. God fulfilled his part of the deal; my relationship with him grew deeper. He filled me with an overwhelming desire to get well!

Thank you, God, that I learned to love you more because of this eat-ing disorder.

Yes, I have loved you with an everlasting love;
Therefore with lovingkindness I have drawn you.

—Jer. 31:3

For six years bingeing and purging was the way I dealt with life. Food was always there when people let me down. I knew the Lord, but he seemed distant and untouchable.

Early in life I had learned that tears were only for the weak, and smiles were just for show on Sunday. I had built a wall around my heart to protect it from the chaos in our home. Performance earned me praise, and love was shallow in my family.

I created my own world where dreams were alive and goodness flourished. I now realize that God lit that flame of hope within me. He and I kept it burning until he placed me with people it was safe to feel with again.

I always sensed that someday things would be different, so I held on to my dreams of love, my sensitive spirit, my rainbow.

Through all the pain of my life God's love was a source of strength. In his time he brought healing and the wisdom to understand the pain. I no longer feel like a lost child whose parents could not show love. I am deeply loved and cherished by my Father in heaven. He is the perfect, loving parent.

God, thank you for the gift of your unchanging love.

*Then Samuel took a stone and set it up between
Mizpah and Shen, and called its name Ebenezer,
saying, "Thus far the LORD has helped us."*
—1 Sam. 7:12

In Old Testament times, after a great victory the Israelites would raise up a stone monument to the Lord. The monument usually consisted of a single stone, called an Ebenezer, which was meant to be a reminder of God's faithfulness. Literally the word means "thus far the Lord has helped us."

I have raised up many emotional Ebenezers in my recovery. After going through a really rough time, I sometimes build a little monument in my mind to remind me of the victory I experienced. Sometimes I journal about the event, but often the occasion is burned so deeply in my heart that there is no need to write it down; it lives on in my memory.

It has been vital to my recovery to remember all the victories. What I glean from one experience often helps me over the next difficult hurdle. I want to be reminded that God has been with me along the way and has worked wonders in my life.

I can't always look to the past; doing that can keep me from moving forward. It helps to glance back at all the little monuments I have raised, and say with a joyful heart, "Thus far the Lord has helped me."

Father, never let me lose sight of how far I've come with your help.

> *Fear not, for I am with you;*
> *Be not dismayed, for I am your God.*
> *I will strengthen you,*
> *Yes, I will help you,*
> *I will uphold you with My righteous*
>   *right hand.*
>
>   —Isa. 41:10

My life has been ruled by fears: the fear of not pleasing everyone, the fear of not being perfect, the fear of rejection. The list goes on.

When God spoke to me through this verse, I realized that he is with me in every situation. We walk together, God and I! I do not have to fear because God is my strength. I know that even when I am not perfect, God still loves me.

With bulimia I reached for food to make me feel safe. Then God showed me that my way of working things out was not his plan for me. He never left me, but he did allow me to make my own decisions.

If you are afraid, don't give up! God loves you. He is there beside you, waiting for you to ask him for help.

Dear Lord, I praise you for never turning away and for strengthening me in my walk of recovery.

The LORD is good,
A stronghold in the day of trouble;
And He knows those who trust in Him.
                                    —Nah. 1:7

I used to believe that once I was free from my eating disorder I would automatically make right choices and nothing bad would happen to me. You see, I thought being bulimic was the reason I had disappointments and failures. I believed those obstacles were a punishment from God for my being bulimic.

Since then, I've learned that sometimes bad things just happen! Disappointments are simply a part of life. I don't always make perfect decisions. Occasionally I really blow it and hurt someone I care about in the process. I have also discovered that being in control of my circumstances has little to do with the number of struggles I face.

When I am experiencing trials and tribulations I know I don't have to handle it on my own. The Lord is with me; he shelters me and helps me get through the pain I must endure. I can take refuge in him, for he alone is my sanctuary.

Father, I thank you for seeing me through the storms of life.

> *And I will have mercy on her who had not*
> *obtained mercy; then I will say to those who were*
> *not My people, "You are My people!" And they*
> *shall say, "You are my God!"*
> —Hos. 2:23

Guilt was the number one factor that kept me addicted to food. A voice inside my head would say, "Go ahead, binge again. You've already ruined your day." I could not seem to get past the thoughts about what I'd done. It overwhelmed me, and a sense of hopelessness washed away my joy.

When I entered treatment I got my first taste of God's forgiveness. It changed my life forever. I learned that if I confess my sins, God will be faithful to forgive me and cleanse me (1 John 1:9).

Before recovery I felt as though all my mistakes were heaped on top of me. I beat myself up for each new one because I had never let go of all the others. I now realize that if I fall, I can get right back up and thank God for his mercy.

I need God's mercy! I want him to see me as pure, and he does because he forgives me.

Thank you, Lord, for not keeping records of my sins.

Wait on the LORD: be of good courage, and he shall strengthen thine heart: wait, I say, on the LORD.
—Ps. 27:14 KJV

In February 1990, we admitted a severely malnourished anorectic in her early thirties. Her body had been ravaged by the disease; her beautiful blue eyes hauntingly pleaded for help. Her trust in the Lord was remarkable in spite of her condition.

Her medical needs and her physical inability to participate in the program at Remuda Ranch meant we had to discharge her. She was transferred to a nursing home, and it appeared that she would soon die. As we prayed together on her last afternoon at the Ranch, she said she liked a bracelet I was wearing. I asked her to take it and bring it back someday.

In September 1991, I was going through a time of spiritual despair. My patience was wearing thin. It seemed that God was ignoring my prayers. Then my phone rang. A strong, healthy voice said, "Hi, I'm in town, and I'd like to see you!"

It was the same woman! When she met me to return my bracelet, I was gratified to see that she looked wonderful.

Father, I thank you for concrete reminders of answered prayers. Please use me according to your will, not mine.

> *Finally, brethren, whatever things are true,*
> *whatever things are noble, whatever things are*
> *just, whatever things are pure, whatever things*
> *are lovely, whatever things are of good report,*
> *if there is any virtue and if there is anything*
> *praiseworthy—meditate on these things.*
> —Phil. 4:8

I hate myself." "I'm fat, ugly, and stupid." "I'm a failure." "God made a mistake when he made me." For years these were the thoughts I dwelt on constantly. Is it any wonder that I hated myself?

When the apostle Paul penned this letter to the Philippians, he gave me an important key to recovery. I cannot walk the path of healing unless I change the way I think.

Dwelling in my self-hatred destroys my confidence. The more I tell myself that I am a failure, the more I see failure in everything I do. That makes it so hard to take risks! If I tell myself that making me was God's mistake, how can I fully trust God with my life?

It helps to stop thinking these negative thoughts, but I need to replace them with something positive. I choose to dwell on the things that are good, true, lovely, and praiseworthy about myself.

Lord, today help me dwell on the good in me.

For son dishonors father,
Daughter rises against her mother,
Daughter-in-law against her mother-in-law;
A man's enemies are the men of his own household.
Therefore, I will look to the LORD;
I will wait for the God of my salvation;
My God will hear me.

—Mic. 7:6–7

When the ones who are supposed to help you and keep you safe hurt you instead, what do you do? I expect my family to guide me and love me, but these things do not happen. Horrible, ugly, painful things take place at home.

I just shut it all inside of me. I plaster on a smile, put on my public face, and go out to face the world. Nobody knows my shame, my fears, or my hatred. At least that was my plan.

It didn't work. I was so filled with hatred and pain that I could not nourish myself. The lies were eating me alive; I couldn't keep up the front. My masks were crumbling around me.

Facing my pain and anger was the hardest thing I ever had to do. I looked constantly to the Lord for his strength and his love. The Lord became my caretaker, my family, and my salvation.

Lord, thank you for being with me. I pray that you will protect every hurting child and adult. Let them find your love and become part of your family.

> *Put my tears into Your bottle;*
> *Are they not in Your book?*
> —Ps. 56:8

Before I developed an eating disorder I spent a lot of time in tears. Many of those tears were for the loneliness I felt. I also shed many tears in anger at myself. I hated myself because I felt I was fat, ugly, and stupid. Other tears were from the intense pain I felt.

Because I was shamed for crying, I learned to turn off the tears and control my feelings. When I caved in and cried, I despised myself for losing control and allowing my weakness to show.

My eating disorder was not just about my fear of becoming fat. Bulimia was the only way I knew to deal with my pain without crying. I learned to stuff the pain and turn off the tears. My eating disorder numbed the ache inside. Focusing on food, weight, or exercise helped me deny my pain and feel in control.

I eventually realized that I had completely shut off my emotions. I was no longer able to feel or cry. My healing began when I decided to stop stuffing the pain with food and to allow myself to cry.

Thank you, Lord, that my tears are precious to you.

He has made everything beautiful in its time.
—Eccl. 3:11

From my perspective things don't look too hopeful right now! I have been out of treatment for my eating disorder for almost one year. I had such high hopes for things—too high, I think. I had convinced myself that all my problems were the result of the disease; now I realize that's not the case.

It was just wishful thinking to count on all my pain being gone once I got my eating under control. I have been reminded again and again that eating disorders are not about food! The abuse of my body and of food was the manifestation of much deeper wounds.

God is in the process of remaking me. I thought it was going to be a simple remodeling job, but it has turned out to be major construction. My thought processes have had to be revamped. This is not a slight adjustment in my life; I'm being completely overhauled!

I get little glimpses of what is to come. The tiny flicker of hope is fed by the baby steps I'm taking these days. Not everything about me is as ugly as it used to be! Some of the anger is gone, and I know the source of what's left. At times I really believe that I am lovable and acceptable to God and that is a real change!

Father, give me patience as I go through this process.

> *He is a double-minded man, unstable in all*
> *his ways.*
> —James 1:8

It has been hard for me to truly give my weight over to God. I spent so many years telling him that I want to turn everything over to him, yet I hold on to this one piece of my life.

A double-minded person is one whose allegiance is divided. I love God, but I love the idea of having a perfect body even more.

Being double-minded is like trying to be a capitalist and a communist, or a Christian and a Buddhist, at the same time. It doesn't make any sense! How can I pledge allegiance to both Christ and Buddha? Eventually I will be so confused by the two doctrines that I will no longer be able to give myself to either one.

You really can trust that God knows what weight is healthiest for you! If you want to give him your life, give it all to him. Otherwise you will be torn between what God wants and what you think is best for you.

───────────

Lord, please help me to give my whole being to you.

Delight yourself also in the LORD,
And He shall give you the desires of your heart.
—Ps. 37:4

I thought this verse was a great way to manipulate God into giving me a perfect body. I would delight myself in him by going to church, worshiping him, and praying. If I did all that, I thought he would bless my desire to be skinny.

To delight myself in God is somewhat like delighting myself in my husband. I spend lots of time with him, talking, listening, and finding out what he enjoys. I tell him what I like and we work toward blending our ideas.

I've learned that to delight myself in God I need to spend time with him and share my desires with him. He listens! And I've found that if I take time to listen long enough, he tells me what his plans are for me.

True, I wanted a perfect body, but he wanted to bring about changes on the inside. I discovered that what I look like on the outside is just not as important as what I'm like on the inside.

As I've learned to delight myself in the Lord, my desires have changed. I can trust him to give me the true desires of my heart. He never fails!

Father, thank you for refining my desires into what you want for me.

> *Two are better than one, . . .*
> *For if they fall, one will lift up his companion.*
> *But woe to him who is alone when he falls,*
> *For he has no one to help him up.*
> —Eccl. 4:9–10

For many months I have overcome my fears and asked for help, because I knew that my life depended upon it. I do not believe I could have progressed this far in my recovery without relying on people for support.

All of a sudden it has become very difficult to share my pain! I came to the point where I admitted I was powerless to heal myself of bulimia. That made it acceptable for me to call a friend for help. I felt justified in asking for support when I struggled with any pain connected to the eating disorder.

Now my pain is of a different brand. I am in big trouble with my marriage. In my mind, it's like starting all over. I now realize that on my own I have no power to have healthy relationships.

I remember feeling so inadequate when I first admitted my eating was out of control. I believed that I should be able to fix the problem. I feel the same way now with my marriage crisis. Again my life is unmanageable, and I must choose to take the problem to God and ask those around me for support. Here I go again!

Father, give me the courage to ask for help.

I can do all things through Christ who strengthens me.
                                        —Phil. 4:13

This verse says that I can do all things through Christ who strengthens me. I have a hard time believing that; it doesn't feel true. But I believe God's Word is true, so that must mean the things I am struggling with are doable with Christ's strength.

Part of the healing process is changing my thoughts. It is more helpful to say, "This is tough, it hurts, but with God's help I can get through it," than to mope and groan and try to avoid my problems.

There is no hope if I battle life alone, but with God's power, I can overcome my eating disorder! My marriage is a wreck, but it's not too big a job for God to handle. The fears I face sending my children off to school each day threaten to swamp me. But with God's peace I can let them go and not obsess about their safety all day long. Finances are always a problem, but my God is big enough to guide us in our spending!

There is no hope for getting through life's daily pain on my own, but with his strength, I can do all things!

Father, teach me to believe that I can do all things through you. Give me strength to face each day.

Cleanse me from secret faults.
—Ps. 19:12

I entered treatment almost one year ago. During my stay, I came clean with many horrible secrets. I shared things that I had never told anyone in my life, shameful things that had been done to me, as well as bad things that I had done.

Since that time, I have made changes in many areas of my life. I have been willing to let go of many of the masks that I wore to please people. The facade of being able to do anything and handle any stress was smashed to bits. I learned that keeping up that front had been very costly.

Recently I realized that there were still areas of my life in which I was not true to myself. I was still trying to put on a show for those around me. These masks are now coming off.

All my life God has known what I was really like on the inside. He saw my pain as I struggled with an eating disorder for thirteen years. He knew of sexual abuse in my past when I had not even dealt with it on a conscious level. God knows all the little secrets that I think I have hidden.

Although revealing my secrets has been painful, there has been a real sense of relief each time I have unloaded a pile. I want to be clean inside, and I long for God to free me from all my secrets.

Father, bring me to the place where I am clean in those secret places.

"And I, if I am lifted up from the earth, will draw
all peoples to Myself."
—John 12:32

I find myself getting caught up in trying to control and manipulate people. I have an internal list of things I think they should be doing, and even how they should be doing them. I even pray that they will understand the truths I know.

My thoughts are not so selfish; I would love to spare them the pain and struggles I have had to face. I think, "If they would only listen to me, they could circumvent many problems!" Can I really spare them?

Spending so much time on other people relieves me of having to deal with myself. If I obsess about the shortcomings I see in others, it distracts me from looking at the flaws in myself.

At church we pass a basket to collect the gifts and offerings. I would never dream of removing my gift from the basket once I placed it there.

Today I can envision myself writing down the name of each person I care for and lovingly placing it in a basket for God. I will remind myself that once I have given that name to the Lord, I have no need to remove it; they're best left in his care.

Lord, help me learn to trust you to care for my loved ones. Help me believe that you will show them the way, and that you will draw them to you.

POWERFUL WORDS

Words of hurt,
Words of pain,
Flung out in anger
Never can be regained.

Words of sorrow,
Words of regret,
Held deep inside
Promises, never to be met.

Words of love,
Like a pleasing balm
Soothing the hurt,
Restoring the calm.

Words of apology,
So hard to say,
Promise a new beginning.
Forgiveness, there is only one way.

> *He brought them out of darkness and the*
> *shadow of death,*
> *And broke their chains in pieces.*
> —Ps. 107:14

I can really relate to darkness, and I have been in the shadow of death many times. Depression and despair were my constant companions during the thirteen years that I struggled with an eating disorder. I lived in a prison of fear and insecurity, and I had no hope of ever breaking free of the cycle of bingeing and purging. All my attempts to stop my self-destructive behavior had failed.

Now, eight months out of treatment, I am able to say that God has broken away the chains that nearly cost me my life. I am on the road to recovery because of his love for me!

Food is no longer the central focus of my life. I am free to use my time and energy doing the things I was created to do. My roles of mother, wife, and friend no longer take a back seat to my eating disorder. There is hope of breaking free from the pain and darkness of addictive habits!

Father, thank you for the reminder of where I've been. It makes where I am going look that much better.

I will bless the Lord who counsels me; he gives me wisdom in the night. He tells me what to do. I am always thinking of the Lord; and because he is so near, I never need to stumble or to fall.

—Ps. 16:7–8 TLB

I search for God's will for my life. What's right? I desire to do what God wants for me, that which is best for my physical, emotional, and spiritual needs. I invest time investigating, planning, and organizing my life, looking for perfection in my own wisdom. Then I pray for God to bless my efforts.

I've got the system all backwards. It works best when I first lay my life at the foot of the cross and seek God's will. He gives me direction for my life.

I've heard it said that "God's will is not rules, but a relationship; it's not a life map, but a lifestyle." I've found that doing what God wants for me does not involve a magical feeling or formula. I'm in his will when I am relying on my relationship with Jesus Christ for my worth.

It is so comforting to know that I do not have to worry about my future as a healthy individual. God promises that he has a good plan for me, and hope for my future (Jer. 29:11)!

His will for me is an expression of his deep love for me; that gives me hope in times of loneliness and discouragement.

God, teach me to turn to you for the answers. I give you control of my life.

> *"And you shall know the truth, and the truth shall make you free."*
> —John 8:32

In trying to protect my emotions and feel secure, I developed my own truth to live by. I made decisions based on distorted perceptions and misinformation which became the foundation for my entire belief system.

I felt compelled to adhere to my self-imposed rules for life. My firm commitment to my own truth gave me the identity I was desperately searching for.

My devotion to my truth seemed both liberating and tormenting. It felt powerful to believe that I didn't need food to live, while others couldn't live without it. But it was agony to feel excluded from God's unconditional love that I knew applied to everyone else.

Having rejected reality, the only absolute in my life was my own truth. However, this caused such inner turmoil and conflict that it eventually brought me to my knees before God, searching for answers.

When I read John 8:32 I had to ask myself, "Does my truth set me free or keep me in bondage?" I realized that there is no substitute for the truth of God's Word. His truth has truly protected me from myself and set me free!

God, give me the wisdom to recognize truth!

Do not lay up for yourselves treasures on earth, where moth and rust destroy and where thieves break in and steal; but lay up for yourselves treasures in heaven, where neither moth nor rust destroys and where thieves do not break in and steal.
—Matt. 6:19–20

I spend a whole lot of time and energy gathering up things to make myself feel better about who I am.

Since I am not acting out in my eating disorder, shopping is another way I numb my feelings. It is easy to get caught up in the search for just the right frame for that picture on my wall. I busy myself looking for bargains in the clothes stores. When I am feeling really insecure, a trip to the grocery store will do the trick. I gain a false sense of security when I see the food filling my cupboards to capacity.

I find myself longing for a new car; that would make life easier for me, I think. Maybe what this family needs is a fun-filled vacation to take the place of love and warmth! My dog is evidence of my attempts to fill the void in my life.

Nice things are just that—nice. But what am I purchasing now that will last? I am usually so busy shopping for things that I miss opportunities to put effort into things that will be left when I am gone.

Father, help me pour myself into things that will last.

> *Dear brothers, is your life full of difficulties and temptations? Then be happy, for when the way is rough, your patience has a chance to grow. So let it grow, and don't try to squirm out of your problems. For when your patience is finally in full bloom, then you will be ready for anything, strong in character, full and complete.*
>
> —James 1:2–4 TLB

I have a hard time finding joy in trials, but Christ instructs me to do that very thing. As I recall the events of the past few years, I am thankful that God gave me the strength to endure. I am now able to see how much I've grown through the battle with my eating disorder. I am closer to God and more mature for having persevered through the difficulties.

Problems are inevitable, and God has a purpose for them. He desires to strengthen my faith in him, develop my endurance, and increase my level of maturity.

The way I choose to respond to problems determines if the situation will control me or if I am able to overcome with God's help. By asking him for help I gain strength and peace.

I am reminded that God has given me strength to cope with problems in the past; that gives me hope about the pain I'm facing now!

Thank you, Lord, for giving me strength, peace, and joy as I face life's daily struggles.

> *But if we hope for what we do not see, we eagerly*
> *wait for it with perseverance.*   —Rom. 8:25

Perseverance—what's that? Part of my distorted thinking is that I should always have what I want when I want it! I got immediate relief from bingeing, purging, or taking a tranquilizer. My emotional pain was such that I could not imagine waiting for things to improve.

In treatment I also wanted things to happen quickly. I especially wanted to get rid of the distorted view I had of my body. I wanted to accept how God had created me. As my body assumed its natural proportions, I prayed that I could someday accept it as being beautiful.

It has taken over one year! Now when I look in the mirror, I see curves where they belong. I feel comfortable in my new clothing size. It happened because I wanted it to. I quit criticizing my body and thanked God for creating me uniquely and in his image.

Take time to appreciate your own unique beauty! Make the decision to persevere and hope for the things you do not yet have.

God, let me see myself as you see me.

> *Therefore, if anyone is in Christ, he is a new creation; old things are passed away; behold, all things have become new.*
> —2 Cor. 5:17

Today I am facing a lot of pain that seems too big for me to handle. In the fear of the moment, I want to escape, to get away from the pain. All at once, things seem overwhelming.

There's nothing new about all this pain. What is new is my response to life's difficulties. Before I entered treatment for my eating disorder, my reaction to pain was to abuse food. Numbing myself by restricting my intake or bingeing and purging was a way to relieve myself of dealing with life. It was extremely difficult to face issues head-on with my head stuck in the toilet.

Right now major areas of my life are completely out of my control. I am in intense pain and I would love to be free of it, if only for a little while. But because of new information that I received in treatment, I'm different! I realize that focusing on food does not make anything change; the problems still exist even when I use food to avoid them.

Abstinence does not keep me pain-free, but it does allow me to choose healthier options for dealing with life.

———————

Father, thank you for making me new.

And have put on the new man who is renewed in knowledge according to the image of Him who created him.

—Col. 3:10

Recovery has brought change to all areas of my life. One of the most difficult changes to deal with is my changing body.

People comment on the difference in my appearance, perhaps because of the obvious contrast to how unhealthy I used to be. I have had to become somewhat tough-skinned and learn to let insensitive remarks roll right off me.

I am also trying to learn to accept the sincere compliments with care. Even the positive comments are hard to hear. I often find myself reading between the lines; it's so hard to believe anything good about myself.

My reaction to comments on my body depends on my interpretation. I can make myself crazy over the most innocent remark! Since I believed that gaining weight equaled failure, I felt humiliated when others pointed out the changes in my body.

To avoid being preoccupied with my body, I'm trying to change my focus. I see myself in the process of becoming a new creation; I can let go of my old beliefs and allow the new me to emerge. I do look different, but the most important changes are in my thoughts, beliefs, and feelings.

Father, help me learn to love this new creation.

> *Be of good courage,*
> *And He shall strengthen your heart,*
> *All you who hope in the LORD.*
> —Ps. 31:24

Reaching out takes courage! It's a big risk that carries with it many fears. Asking for help means admitting to others that I am not perfect, that I have needs, and that I don't have all the answers. It means letting down the walls I have built around myself.

One year ago I realized that I had to ask for help. It was a choice between life and death. I gathered up every ounce of courage within me and made the decision to admit that I was sick.

That choice allowed me to enter treatment for my eating disorder. It was a big risk, but the reward for being courageous enough to ask for help was life!

After taking that first step it became easier to take risks. I found the strength to move out of an unhealthy environment to a new city where I knew only one person! There I forced myself to get involved with people and make friends. I never dreamed that I was capable of having honest, open, intimate relationships.

Because I had the courage, God gave me the strength to plow through the feelings of awkwardness and loneliness. He helped me live through the fears that I thought I could never face. People have accepted me for who I am, and the fears have begun to fade.

Father, thank you for providing me with the courage to live. Continue to give me strength!

I will praise You, O LORD, with my whole heart;
I will tell of all Your marvelous works.
I will be glad and rejoice in You;
I will sing praise to Your name, O Most High.
—Ps. 9:1–2

In the depths of depression, the last thing I feel like doing is praising the Lord; it seems too hard! However, I don't praise him because I feel like it, but because of who he is.

I can't imagine that David felt much like praising God when he was surrounded by enemies who intended to kill him, but he did it anyway. Like David, I can offer my praise as a sacrifice to the Lord, in spite of my circumstances.

Listening to inspirational music helps to quiet my heart. I usually feel an immediate change in my spirit when I listen to it. Since my body follows the signals it receives from my mind and my heart, my physical being is enhanced as well.

God can replace my depression with the desire to praise him. He chases away my sorrow and fills me with a joy that only comes from him!

Lord, no matter how I feel, I will praise you!

He will feed His flock like a shepherd;
He will gather the lambs with His arm,
And carry them in His bosom,
And gently lead those who are with young.
—Isa. 40:11

My name is Sandy, and I'm a mom. I think there ought to be a group called "Moms Anonymous" for those perfectionistic moms who can't let go of the little stuff. I can see myself beating my eating disorder, but I can't visualize myself as a competent mother.

No matter what I do, it doesn't seem good enough! My two little girls are healthier and happier now that they've got a recovering mom. They're doing fine, yet I agonize over the mistakes I make. Why am I so hard on myself? I'm rarely as critical of anyone else.

God loves my children, and he carries them close to his heart. My heavenly Father sees me as one of his flock, too. He gently leads those who have young.

It is a good feeling to know that my Father leads me gently. He corrects my mistakes by lovingly redirecting me to the fold. If God is not harsh with me, then I don't have to beat up on myself. I can put away my sledgehammer and trust him to help me put my mothering in perspective. I may be a mother sheep, but I'm also one of his lambs.

Teach me to be gentle with myself, Lord.

*Having predestined us to adoption as sons by Jesus
Christ to Himself, according to the good pleasure of
His will.*
—Eph. 1:5

I came from a dysfunctional family; my earthly parents were not able to give me what I needed emotionally. My parents carried pain from their own parents, and that prevented them from providing me with what I needed.

I grew up watching the perfect families on television. I dreamed of being part of one of those families; I wanted to have perfect parents like the ones portrayed on TV. I found that I was angry and resentful at my parents for not being perfect.

I finally realized that my parents don't have to be perfect; God is my heavenly Father, and he is perfect. He loves me like no one else could ever love me! In fact, he loves me with the same kind of love he had for his Son Jesus. God has adopted me into his family, and he is able to meet all my needs.

I am now free to love my parents for who they are. I am thankful for the love and care they were able to give me; I don't need them to be perfect anymore!

Father, I praise you for adopting me into your family.

> *But rejoice to the extent that you partake of Christ's
> sufferings, that when His glory is revealed, you may
> also be glad with exceeding joy.*
>   —1 Peter 4:13

I probably read this verse about fifty times before I realized what it meant. I had always struggled to get out of painful situations, but God was showing me that the pain was there for a reason.

He spoke these words to my heart: "Yes, there will be many trials and tribulations during your life. There will be times you wonder if you will survive the pain; you'll feel like giving up! Remember, my child, that I also suffered greatly. When glory comes, the joy we will share will be beyond your dreams."

In my mind, if my life was perfect in every way, why would I look forward to heaven?

Precious Jesus, do you see my pain? I feel like I might go insane. Please rise this day and swell my heart; Satan has pierced it with his poisonous dart. My life is unmanageable and out of control; down and down I've gone until my heart is black as coal. It feels like there is no one to lean on or depend. Is there someone you know to send? I've lost my way in this black hole; send your Holy Spirit to fill my soul. Release me from my want and ache, so I may live in glory for your sake!

For thus says the high and exalted One
Who lives forever, whose name is Holy,
"I dwell on a high and holy place,
And also with the contrite and lowly of spirit
In order to revive the spirit of the lowly
And to revive the heart of the contrite."
—Isa. 57:15 NASV

I am lowly of spirit and broken before the Lord. I feel alone and abandoned by everyone around me. I long to pour out my heart, but the words elude me. Who will listen to my pain?

My Father is magnificent! He doesn't look down at me from his high and holy places; He is with me in my brokenness. Everyone else may have abandoned me, but God is with me.

At times when I retreat from those who love me, I try to withdraw from God, too. I may try to ignore him, but he does not ignore me! He knows me and feels my pain and despair.

It is hard for me to accept these truths about God. Why does he want to be with me when I am in the depths of despair? I don't like to be near people in pain; it's too much of a downer!

God's love for me is unfathomable; I can't compare it with my limited ability to love. He wants to revive my spirit and heal my heart!

Dear Father, thank you for being with me in the pits as well as when I'm on the mountaintop.

"Come to Me, all you who labor and are heavy laden, and I will give you rest. Take My yoke upon you and learn from Me, for I am gentle and lowly in heart, and you will find rest for your souls. For My yoke is easy and My burden is light."

—Matt. 11:28–30

I am so tired! This eating disorder wears me out. I keep saying that I will do better, but I fall back into the same old habits over and over again.

Today I ate less than my food plan and exercised more than I should have. What's wrong with me? I hate myself for doing these things. I know that acting out with food does not change any of the things that are really bothering me.

I am once again at the point where I have to ask God for help. All I have to do is come to him, and he has promised to give me rest.

Thinking these thoughts brings a smile to my face. I feel more positive and secure now. The burden of this eating disorder is too heavy for me to carry all alone, but with Jesus there to help it becomes a little lighter.

I know every day will not be perfect, but resting in Jesus, I know I can make it!

Thank you, Father, for the rest I find in you!

But those who wait on the Lord
Shall renew their strength;
They shall mount up with wings like eagles,
They shall run and not be weary,
They shall walk and not faint.

—Isa. 40:31

Sometimes I feel imprisoned by the pressure placed on me by myself and others. Happiness seems to be far off in the future, at the end of a never-ending list of things to do. This list ranges from succeeding at work to getting married. It also includes avoiding conflict, helping others, dressing perfectly, and maintaining my ideal weight.

I am worn out from trying to meet such high expectations! I long for freedom. I want to be free now, not someday after I have achieved certain goals. Do you feel the pressure to perform?

I read in this verse that I can find strength in the Lord. My challenge is to wait on him for my power. I have to give up the delusion that some act I may accomplish will give me what I need.

Imagine running and not getting tired. In the state I am in, it is hard to dream of walking and not fainting. But I long to soar through each new day! I choose to wait on the Lord for his power.

Father, give me the strength to wait on you!

> *For we have no power against this great multitude*
> *that is coming against us; nor do we know what to*
> *do, but our eyes are upon You. . . . Do not be*
> *afraid nor dismayed because of this great*
> *multitude, for the battle is not yours, but God's.*
> —2 Chron. 20:12b, 15b

This Scripture is about a period of distress in Israel's history. The Israelites were facing a great multitude of enemies who wanted to drive them out of the land that the Lord had given them. They were overwhelmed and did not know what to do.

They looked to the Lord in their time of trouble. He spoke to them and told them not to be fearful because it was his battle. When the Israelites went to meet the enemy, they found only corpses! The Lord had done it all!

I found so much strength in this story. I have had to face many battles with my eating disorder. It seemed like no matter where I looked, there was another enemy trying to destroy me.

I found that unless I admitted I was powerless, there was no chance for victory. As long as I tried to fight the battle on my own, I was crushed. At the end of my strength, God was there with all his mighty power! I finally gave up and allowed him to do battle against my enemy.

Lord, remind me to look to you when I am facing the enemy.

Now I rejoice, not that you were made sorry, but that your sorrow led to repentance. For you were made sorry in a godly manner, that you might suffer loss from us in nothing. For godly sorrow produces repentance leading to salvation, not to be regretted; but the sorrow of the world produces death.
—2 Cor. 7:9–10

When I reflect on my battle with eating disorders, I often begin to feel bleak. I wonder, "Why me, God?" But then I am always reminded of the results of that eating disorder.

I now have a wonderful new relationship with God. I have also learned to let go of unhealthy relationships, and my hunger for money and power no longer controls my life. I have actually learned to like myself! These changes in my life all occurred because of my eating disorder. In seeking help for that disease, I was given the tools I needed to live a healthy, productive life.

Now, as I head toward an exciting new career and new life in God, I am thankful for my eating disorder. It has given me a second chance at life, this time as a human being, not a human doing!

Father, thank you for the changes in my life.

And now, Lord, what do I wait for?
My hope is in You.   —Ps. 39:7

Oh, no! I've done it again. I crawled into the "hopeless boat." I tossed the life jacket overboard, threw away the oars, and floated out into the sea of despair.

When I'm feeling down, it is so easy to isolate myself, to skip my support groups, to quit reaching out by phone. I make a choice to start sliding down the slippery path to relapse. It's that simple—a choice!

I know the answers. When I lose hope, that is the time to beef up my recovery plan. It is so hard to get out of the house to be with people when all I want to do is crawl under the covers and hide. It's easier to let the machine answer all the calls so I can keep telling myself, "No one cares if I live or die."

The next time I see the "hopeless boat" docking, I want to make sure I do all I can to ensure that it doesn't drop anchor. I can gain hope attending groups where there are others who understand me. I can share with another person that I am hurting and lonely. I read in his Word that God loves me and values me! These things bring hope!

Father, give me the courage to do what I need to do when I feel hopeless.

*For to everyone who has, more will be given, and
he will have abundance; but from him who does
not have, even what he has will be taken away.*
—Matt. 25:29

God blessed me with gifts and strengths, but I was
rarely satisfied with the way I used them. I found fault
with everything I attempted. I attributed my dissatisfaction to the fact that my body was imperfect. I believed that my life would be ideal if only I were thinner.

Gradually I took fewer risks. I thought, "If I can't do
it perfectly, why bother?" I put more effort into becoming thinner, as if that would solve all my problems.

As I became more obsessed with looking perfect, I
grew more unwilling to take risks. If I could not be assured that my efforts would result in perfection, I
chose not to try. I couldn't try; I was paralyzed by my
fear of failure!

One day God stirred my heart with thoughts of what
I was doing with the talents he had given me. I realized
that, much like the servant of this passage, I had buried
my gifts because of my fears (Matt. 25:25).

I wasted many opportunities to give of myself over
the years because I feared people more than God. I
desired my glory instead of his. If God is pleased with
my efforts, why should I be ashamed of them?

*Dear Jesus, keep me from burying all that you have given me under a
pile of fear.*

He who dwells in the secret place of the Most High
Shall abide under the shadow of the Almighty.
I will say of the LORD, "He is my refuge and my fortress;
My God, in Him I will trust."
Surely He shall deliver you from the snare of the fowler
And from the perilous pestilence.
He shall cover you with His feathers,
And under His wings you shall take refuge;
His truth shall be your shield and buckler.

—Ps. 91:1–4

Today is another one of those days. My head feels foggy; inwardly I feel jittery and unsure. The day looks long and difficult. How will I make it through another day in this battle against my eating disorder?

There is a dark cloud all around me; the storm of feelings is raging within. Where are you, God? Have you left me to fight this storm alone? I don't have the strength!

I look for the rainbow, but all around me are dark clouds. Please, Lord, shelter and protect me today. Remind me of your faithfulness through the song of the bird or the laughter of children. Today they will be my rainbow, my promise of sunshine ahead.

Father, help me remember to seek refuge in you and not in food today.

But the fruit of the Spirit is love, joy, peace,
longsuffering, kindness, goodness, faithfulness.
—Gal. 5:22

The first woman to enter treatment at Remuda Ranch stayed for six months. Her husband and children participated in Family Week, but her parents were reluctant to participate.

God intervened, and her parents agreed to make the trip to Arizona. That was a tough week for the whole family; each individual was faced with hard truths. In the end, it became a gift of love they gave to each other.

The year after treatment was not easy for that first resident. It seemed that the misery would never end, but the love, trust, and faith that family had in the Lord prevailed!

When they visited the Ranch this fall, it was such an encouragement to see her. She was at normal weight and glowing with health! The entire family is enjoying a new close and loving relationship. The fruit is becoming evident.

———————

Praise you, Jesus. Thank you for answered prayers.

> *I shall not die, but live,*
> *And declare the works of the LORD.*
> —Ps. 118:17

This verse jumped out at me one day when I was wishing for death to put an end to all my fears, anxieties, and depression. The uncertainty of the future made me cling to food in order to gain control.

I did not see the point in choosing life when it was so painful. I felt worthless and hopeless, and I was constantly depressed. I struggled with my fears about how my eating disorder and emotional instability would scar my children.

As I considered what the verse said, God showed me some things. As a woman with an eating disorder, I can help others turn toward God as he heals me from this disease. If I choose to live, my progress in recovery can be a statement to those who have witnessed my struggles that God is faithful and powerful.

I have the opportunity to proclaim what God has done in my seemingly hopeless life. I can have an impact on my family, children, friends, and others who are caught up in the devastating cycle of eating disorders. In this I can glorify God and find purpose for life.

Thank you, Lord, for giving me the desire and the will to live!

But those who wait on the LORD
Shall renew their strength;
They shall mount up with wings like eagles,
They shall run and not be weary,
They shall walk and not faint.

—Isa. 40:31

Some of my greatest strengths are also my greatest weaknesses. My persistence in getting the job done is a big asset but that attribute does not always work in my favor. I sometimes become compulsive when a task seems impossible.

Many times I push to find an instant solution to problems that are best left to God's timing. I tend to manipulate situations in order to find an easy answer.

I have spent many sleepless nights worrying and planning when God knew the plan all along. I really needed my sleep, and my nocturnal fretting has actually created some big messes!

God is slowly, sometimes painfully, teaching me to wait on him. My first plan of action is now to become aware. I make a conscious effort to put things on the back burner for a few days. It isn't easy, but my perspective often changes after a short wait.

I am choosing to rely on God's strength for my daily responsibilities. I could not stand the load on my own, but I find new power to go on in him.

Father, you know how tired and discouraged I have become because of my compulsive behavior. I want to run and not be weary as I learn to wait on you.

> *Cease to dwell on days gone by and to brood over*
> *past history. Here and now I will do a new thing;*
> *this moment it will break from the bud.*
> —Isa. 43:18–19 TEV

While my daughter was in treatment for her eating disorder, I went through the most grueling, soul-searching week of my life. For a time I truly wished I could die. I wanted to escape the hurt, despair, and rejection that I believed my daughter felt toward me.

I felt responsible for her heartache and misery. Whether it was totally or partially my fault, she was in a great deal of pain. I tried to sort it out in my own mind, alone and with professionals, but could not get much peace or satisfaction. I found myself unable to sleep or to fulfill my roles at home and work.

I could not forget the sadness in my daughter's eyes when she said, "I needed you and you weren't there for me." Then God brought to mind this passage of Scripture; I read it again and again.

I was brooding over what was passed. I saw how God was beginning to work in my daughter's life; he was healing her! It was a slow and painful process, not without a few setbacks, but she was making changes. Now I understand that the Lord was there to see us both through the most difficult time in our lives.

Thank you, Lord, for the privilege of being able to say, "I can't handle this; please take control."

This is a faithful saying: for if we died with Him,
we shall also live with Him. If we endure, we shall
also reign with Him.   —2 Tim. 2:11–12

Many times I have wondered why some people seem to get more than their share of obstacles in life. I've struggled with my eating disorder. I have friends who have been physically and sexually abused. I know children who are neglected by their parents. Why?

As I reflect on this question, I am aware that each experience plays a significant role in developing an individual's character. I met many women in treatment for eating disorders at Remuda Ranch. These ladies told stories that made my heart break.

I am struck by the obstacles my friends have faced and survived. Their experiences increased the depth of their character. Through the pain of life, sensitivity, creativity, and understanding blossomed.

When I think of suffering, I cannot help thinking about Jesus. While on earth he was ridiculed, betrayed, and eventually put to death. He really understands my pain! I remind myself that by enduring what hurts the most, I will reign with Christ one day. Knowing that does not take away the pain, but it does give meaning to it.

Lord, give me the courage to keep up the fight so that I may one day reign with you.

> *Therefore, if anyone is in Christ, he is a new*
> *creation; old things have passed away; behold,*
> *all things have become new.* —2 Cor. 5:17

Sometimes I feel trapped in my past. Even though I am in recovery and I'm moving forward, the process of working through my past can bog me down. What adds to that is the reality that I live in the same house with the same kitchen where I used to binge. I drive the same car that takes me to the same stores where I used to buy huge quantities of food. Sometimes it overwhelms me! No matter where I look, my past is haunting me.

It helps to remind myself that I am new in Christ. He has renewed me! My relationship with him is helping me become a different person than I used to be.

To further my healing, I must look at unpleasant things from my past. But I am not the same. I have a new determination in my mind and a new commitment in my heart. I will allow God to lead me through the pain of my past so that I will be able to live in the newness of today!

God, when I feel caught in the painful memories of my past, I can thank you for helping me become new. Thank you for this clean start at life.

The wise woman builds her house,
But the foolish pulls it down with her hands.
—Prov. 14:1

I was so unhappy and depressed during my first marriage that I divorced my husband. I wanted the pain to stop so that I could be happy. Ten years later I accepted Jesus Christ as my personal Savior.

Since then God has been perfecting me, and it has been very painful. I promised God as I married for the second time that it would be "until death do us part." Subconsciously, I was still looking for a perfect life.

When the depression and unhappiness didn't go away, I began to realize that my expectations were too high. In this second marriage, I have had to face many more difficulties than I did in the first one. I have learned to accept that the perfect life simply does not exist; everyone struggles!

Part of God's design for marriage is that two people bring out the junk in each other so each can become more Christ-like.

Father, I thank you for my husband. I ask your blessing on our marriage as we work through each other's imperfections.

No temptation has overtaken you except such as is common to man; but God is faithful, who will not allow you to be tempted beyond what you are able, but with the temptation will also make the way of escape, that you may be able to bear it.
—1 Cor. 10:13

I was lying on my bed crying. I had been flooded all day with memories from my past. On top of that, several of the professionals I had been working with were suggesting that I change therapists once I got home! I felt like the walls were caving in on me. I had entered treatment voluntarily, and it seemed like all I got for my effort was a lot of pain.

My roommate came in the room. I screamed, "This is too much and I can't take it anymore!" She sat down beside me and said, "Did you see the rainbow outside today? I like to think of rainbows as God's promise that he will not leave my side or give me more than I can handle."

As I thought about the words I grew calm. My thoughts slowed and the memories I had been carrying around all day seemed less intense. I realized that God had spoken through my roommate's words and had filled me with a sense of peace.

Thank you, God, for not giving me more than I can bear with your help.

To You, O LORD, I lift up my soul.
O my God, I trust in You;
Let me not be ashamed;
Let not my enemies triumph over me.
—Ps. 25:1–2

The Lord knows my soul. He knows when I am fearful, when I am petty, when I have been hurt, when I feel joyful. He hears my prayers and sees my tears; God loves me.

It is a wondrous gift to have someone who knows the best and the worst about me and loves me anyway. I do trust the Lord with my soul, and I believe he knows how best to care for me.

It is so easy to feel ashamed about the hidden places in my heart. I have struggled to share myself with others, but it is hard to push through the shame. God already knows all the stuff I try to hide, and he still loves me.

I choose to continue to give my soul to the Lord. If I don't, the shame becomes so great that I make poor choices. Abusing my body does not take away my guilt, but for many years, that was the only way I knew to deal with my feelings.

Today, I will give myself to the Lord. He knows all my secrets and he loves me anyway!

Dear Lord, thank you for the gift of your love and acceptance.

TOO FAT!

Too fat, too fat, too fat, the message rings in
my ears.
Layers of self-hatred I built over the years.
To weigh 212, how could this be? I know of
this weight I have to be free.
Trapped in this life is like living in Hell.
Maybe at 194 all will be well.
After I shed the pounds, people would muse:
You look so much better, you needed to lose!
To binge and purge, my life was obsessed.
The pounds have come off, but the hate is
still there. All I can feel is anger and fear.
Then comes the thrill, the energy high. I can
eat all I want, I can reach the sky!
But of course it came to an end, when I felt I
had lost my very best friend.
I said I would stop, but that was a lie. I was
out of control and wanted to die.
My friends and the counselor shout in my
face, "You need to get help; treatment's the
place!"
However, by now my denial's so strong, I
truly believed them all to be wrong.
But a still, small voice from deep down inside
told me my pain I could no longer hide.
The layers of hate I've gained over the years
will have to come off by shedding the tears.

> *The fear of the LORD is the beginning of knowledge,*
> *But fools despise wisdom and instruction.*
>
> —Prov. 1:7

There have been plenty of times during my recovery that I did not want to be told what to do! Although I have worked hard to trust my therapist and others who are helping me, sometimes I just don't want to hear what they have to say.

Often I do not want to change my behavior; things feel comfortable the way they are, even if they aren't healthy. I have made big strides in breaking the old patterns; give me a break!

My eating disorder is no longer taking priority in my life, but there are still plenty of other areas that need attention.

When I am thinking clearly, I know that it is foolish not to work on the new issues in my life. Unfortunately, I do not always think clearly. I choose not to listen to instruction, even when it's given by the people I usually trust.

Today I will try to be wise and listen to the people God has surrounded me with at this time in my life. Being resistant to instruction will only prolong the process of becoming whole.

Lord, remind me when I am being foolish.

This is the day the LORD has made;
We will rejoice and be glad in it.
—Ps. 118:24

Sitting in church one Sunday, I had a difficult time keeping my mind on the service. All I could think about was the shape of my body. I was obsessed with thoughts of my waist, hips, thighs. I started comparing myself with others' shapes around me. Suddenly my thoughts were interrupted.

Directly in front of me were two young, smiling girls. They were singing their hearts out. I was stunned. Unlike me, these girls were not waiting to smile, to sing, or to be happy until they reached their desired weight or shape. They were living life that very moment! They were praising God in that place and at that time.

I often think to myself, "When this flaw is changed, then I will be happy. When that is different then I can get serious about my healing. When I have that under control, then I'll have it made." I need to remember that each day in the process is a day to rejoice.

Lord, give me the courage to accept myself today. I want to focus on you and give you praise for this moment in time.

> *I am with you always, even to the end of the age.*
> —Matt. 28:20

For the first time in my life I am all alone! I went right from my parents' home to my husband's place. I have never been by myself. During the nine weeks I spent in treatment for my eating disorder I was surrounded by people.

It's very scary to be alone for the first time. I was not sure I could do it! Little things like being in the dark are not so little now.

What can I do when I am afraid? Food was always my solace before I began my recovery; I ate to drown out the feelings. But I learned that eating did not take away the things I feared; it only made me numb.

Nevertheless, God is with me, and he is now my comfort. I talk to him when I am afraid or lonely; he is a good listener. I guess I'm not really alone after all!

Lord, please stay close; being alone is scary!

They looked to Him and were radiant,
And their faces were not ashamed.
—Ps. 34:5

During the course of my therapy I learned something that helped me understand myself. I was living under an immense blanket of shame; I was ashamed of my past and continued to feel shame about my present. I always felt guilty, as if I were to blame for everything that happened to everyone. I knew I had always felt that way, I just did not know how to explain it.

I thought I had to be perfect in order to feel less shame. Since perfection was unattainable, no matter how hard I tried I lived in constant shame.

God opened my eyes and showed me the way out of this awful pattern. He led me to this verse; the words were like music to my worn out, perfectionistic heart.

The thought of being radiant instead of feeling ashamed was pleasant to think about. But how could I, with my past, be radiant? As I turned to look to God, he assured me that I indeed was his beautiful daughter whose face glowed with the radiance of his love.

Father, remind me to look to you when the shame overwhelms me.

> *Thou who knowest, O LORD,*
> *Remember me, take notice of me.*
> —Jer. 15:15 NAS

Inside this grown-up recovering bulimic, there is a little girl who is starved for attention. Many of my needs went unmet as a child, and although I look like an adult, my behavior is often childlike.

I used to turn to food for comfort. Food never let me down, but it wasn't very good company. I could fill myself with food, but it didn't take away the loneliness. In fact, eating never took away any of my pain. It merely numbed me to the fact that the pain was still there.

God has always been there, even though that is hard to believe. He remembered me when everyone else forgot. He noticed my sad eyes when my parents did not even know that I had been abused.

My strong need for attention today is hard to handle. My inner needs can be met only by the Lord, but I constantly try to get others to fill them.

"Hey, world, take a look at me! I'm getting better; I am a real person, capable of doing worthwhile things!" Often people are too busy to notice me, but God is there, and he notices. He hasn't forgotten me.

Father, help me to stop seeking attention from others when what I really need is you.

But He was wounded for our transgressions,
He was bruised for our iniquities;
The chastisement for our peace was upon Him,
And by His stripes we are healed.

—Isa. 53:5

The question still repeats itself in my mind. "So you have been healed by the blood of Jesus?" It was a live radio broadcast on the topic of eating disorders. I heard my voice answering weakly, "Yes." And then my chance was over; the broadcast ended. I felt sick instantly! Why had I answered like that? I knew the answer I wanted to give immediately after we were off the air.

Jesus offered me healing much like he made it available to my friend who has cancer. She has had to take an active part in the healing process. She has sought out medical help and pursued many options for treating the disease. My friend has endured the pain of the healing and kept up her desire to live.

I remembered the humiliation I felt when I first admitted that I was bulimic. Even though I was determined to get well, I had many fears about entering treatment. It was painful to face the events in my past that were at the core of my eating disorder.

Yes, I have been healed by the blood of Jesus. But it wasn't an instant cure. He chose to use therapy, doctors, and a treatment center in my healing.

Father, I thank you for my healing.

> *All the days of the afflicted are evil,*
> *But he who is of a merry heart has*
> *a continual feast.*
>
> —Prov. 15:15

While I was practicing my eating disorder, I thought that life was one big problem after another! My thinking was so negative that it was hard to see any good around me. My eyes only saw the pain and ugliness of life.

Since I began my recovery I have started to see things in a different light. Everything seems less bleak now. There are tiny little gaps in the thick layer of pain in my heart; through those I am able to see some of the goodness in life.

Life still has its ups and downs, but there are positive things taking place in me. I choose to hang on to every little achievement. Seeing things more positively helps me to continue.

In the past, the only way I feasted was on food. I drowned my body and mind with excess calories and then had to deal with the guilt and shame I felt afterward. When I chose to relieve myself of the food, more guilt was added to the pile. It was an endless cycle.

These days it is easier to feast on other things. I can choose to enjoy my children as I watch them grow. I find pleasure in the growth that is taking place in my life. Life isn't perfect, but it isn't all bad either!

Father, help me to see the feast you have for me.

*But let patience have its perfect work, that you may
be perfect and complete, lacking nothing.*
—James 1:4

I am amazed by the changes in me! I have enjoyed
nine months of abstinence from disordered eating. Before I entered treatment, I never would have believed I
could refrain from bingeing, purging, and restricting
for even one day. But God is good! He preserved my
life until such a time that I became willing to admit my
need and ask for help.

I can see now that God was there all along. I was just
too busy being angry, feeling victimized, and protecting myself to notice that I was being saved from my
greatest enemy, myself.

God allowed me to be in a place where I was forced
to give up bingeing and purging long enough to deal
with some of the pain and emptiness that led to my
eating disorder.

I'm not settling for just abstinence! It's a great start,
but it's not enough. I want to live and become all that
God planned for me to be. I am so thankful to have this
chance at life without being controlled by food.

Father, help me to be patient while you help me change.

> *Therefore comfort each other and edify one*
> *another, just as you also are doing.*
> —1 Thess. 5:11

Support groups have played such an important part in my recovery from eating disorders! It is an effort to attend each week, but I am always glad to get there. By listening to others, I am able to recognize areas of my own life that still need attention.

Being around people who understand what I am going through is encouraging. It helps to know that I am not the only one in this boat. I gain acceptance for myself as I learn that others are struggling with the same issues I face.

Often I feel like I have made no progress at all. It is easy to see the areas where I am still lacking. My friends in groups are able to see the growth that has taken place. They encourage me by pointing out what changes I've made.

It would be nice not to have to go to support groups, but I still need the comfort I find there. I like to think that others find comfort when I share as well.

God has used people to comfort me and build me up when I feel too weak to continue. I draw upon the encouragement of others. What a gift!

Father, help me continue to build up others and encourage them as they do the same for me.

They have mouths, but they cannot speak;
They have eyes, but they cannot see;
They have ears, but they cannot hear;
They have noses, but they cannot smell;
They have hands, but they cannot feel;
They have feet, but they cannot walk;
They cannot make a sound with their throat.
—Ps. 115:5–7 NAS

This verse is speaking specifically of idols—inanimate objects, things that are not alive. However, when I read it I couldn't help thinking how it described me. For most of my life, I was dead! I was turned off and tuned out, just plain numb.

Today, right now at this very moment, I am alive! I feel normal. Circumstances are neither desperately hopeless nor tremendously exciting. This is life.

It is so amazing to be aware of these things. For thirteen years I used my eating disorder to shield me from feeling anything at all. I existed in a vacuum, convincing myself that it was the only safe way to live. I spent much time and energy protecting myself from painful memories and new hurts.

My heart is full of gratitude for the opportunity I had to be in treatment where it was safe to learn to feel again! I try to remember that it is okay to feel even though I was taught to discount my feelings. I can learn a new way of living.

God, thank you for giving me five senses.

> *Jesus Christ is the same yesterday, today, and forever.*
> —Heb. 13:8

All my life, things have felt out of control! As a victim of sexual abuse, my control was taken away from me. Those events left me feeling very unstable.

My family moved around a lot when I was growing up because my dad changed jobs quite often. It was hard to feel secure when we were always moving from place to place.

My parents' relationship was a constant source of stress in our family. Their constant arguing left an air of tension in the house.

A major factor that led to my eating disorder was the lack of stability in my life. I was fearful and insecure; I longed for something solid and constant in my life.

Now I have found it! Jesus is constant; he is stable. He does not move or change or vary from day to day. He is always with me. It is hard for me to grasp the concept of anything being the same forever, but it gives me hope to know that I have stability because I am connected to him.

This is not one of those deals that sounds too good to be true. There is no catch this time! Jesus is the same; he never changes.

Lord, I am grateful for the stability you bring to my life.

And on the seventh day God ended His work, and
He rested on the seventh day from all His work
which He had done.
—Gen. 2:2

The verses prior to this one in Genesis outline how God created the world. He worked for six days and then he stopped working and rested. How is it that even God the Creator is allowed to rest, but I do not give myself that privilege?

As things become more stressful in my life, I find myself pushing even harder than I normally would. When I am at a breaking point, I work compulsively rather than give myself a much-needed break.

My compulsive drive to work is another form of my illness. I am no longer numbing myself with food, but frantic activity has almost the same effect. If I keep going, I do not have to stop and look at what's hurting inside me.

I have found that my productivity is increased when I take time out to nurture myself. A long walk helps to clear my head. I find a big release in reading a good book. It is much easier to apply myself to the work at hand when I allow time for fun!

As I progress toward wholeness, I am learning to stop and rest. I can take the example from my Creator and allow myself to sit still once in a while.

Father, I pray that you will give me the courage to stop moving long enough to deal with life. Help me learn to have fun!

Who of you by worrying can add a single hour to his life? And why do you worry about clothes? See how the lilies of the field grow. They do not labor or spin.
—Matt. 6:27–28 NIV

Often I can't think of anything but my body. I worry and fret over my weight, my size, my shape, and how I look in my clothes. This one aspect of my eating disorder plagues me.

My tendency to be obsessed with myself drains me of energy that could be spent on life. There is not much left of me to put toward being a mom, a wife, a friend.

If it's true that all behavior serves a purpose, then what function is my self-absorption serving? It definitely keeps me from feeling. It prevents me from carrying out the tasks at hand. It frees me from all responsibility, since I am totally consumed with self. This self-centered routine enables me to remain distant from the possibility of any pain or discomfort.

Sadly, this same behavior also eliminates the possibility of experiencing joy. Being controlled by thoughts of myself stunts my growth both spiritually and emotionally. I am unavailable to God and the work he has laid out for me because my mind is bogged down with the fears and insecurities that come from focusing on my body.

Father, free me from my self-centeredness!

And when the Chief Shepherd appears, you will
receive the crown of glory that does not fade away.
—1 Peter 5:4

I have spent much of my life seeking praise and approval for my achievements. I want people to notice when I do something well. I have been so empty inside that I always had to perform to feel worthwhile.

When I lose weight I wait for comments from others to make myself feel attractive. It isn't enough to know that I have lost the weight. When I start to help someone by sharing, I soon find myself telling others about my accomplishment to gain approval.

My cooking is one area that has always brought the attention I craved, but that very thing also fed the disease that I battled. In order to gain acceptance I made elaborate, expensive meals. That made it easy for me to spend compulsively as well as practice my eating disorder.

All of the compliments and glory I receive here on earth fade away so fast! My need for constant strokes feeds my compulsive drive to perform.

Christ is not going to be interested in how well I cooked or how thin I looked. What is important to him are things that can't even be seen! The rewards I get from him will be based on the performance of my heart; that glory will last!

Lord, help me remember the things I'm capable of that will bring lasting rewards.

> *Therefore I say to you, do not worry about your
> life, what you will eat or what you will drink; nor
> about your body, what you will put on. Is not life
> more than food and the body more than clothing?*
> —Matt. 6:25

Growing up without enough food and clothing has
left some painful scars in my heart. I always wondered
if I had just imagined the lack of essentials in my home
as a child.

During my Family Week in treatment I asked my
brother and sister what their perception was. It was so
affirming to hear them say that they too were aware of
the scarcity of food and clothing. I had just assumed
that it was another case of my overactive imagination.

That reality helped me put a lot of things in perspective. I was able to be kinder to myself knowing that I
really had grown up without knowing where my next
meal was coming from.

I had always been repulsed by my obsession with
food. I was embarrassed by the way I ate. Now God is
gently changing my heart. I know that I won't always
look to food for my security.

God, teach me to trust you for my daily needs.

*These things indeed have an appearance of wisdom
in self-imposed religion, false humility, and neglect
of the body, but are of no value against the
indulgence of the flesh.*
　　　　　　　　　　　　　　　—Col. 2:23

I have been on some pretty strange diets in my lifetime! There were always strict guidelines to follow for
losing weight. No matter how heavy I was, I always felt
deprived when I had to abide by a list of things I was
not permitted to eat.

With as much self-hatred as I had, I almost enjoyed
strict, punishing diets. It made me feel strong to know
that I could do without foods that I normally enjoyed. I
had a sense of accomplishment, even though I felt punished.

Eating in front of others is usually difficult for me,
but when I was on a diet I found sympathy forthcom-
ing! "Poor dear, she can't have any dessert." Those
kinds of comments fed my feelings of false humility. I
also gained a sense of power, knowing that I could resist foods that others craved.

For some time after I left treatment for my eating
disorder, I followed a sensible food plan rigidly. Trusting that food plan gave me a feeling of security during
the time when I struggled to adjust to my new way of
life. Today, I am feeling more free to take risks with my
food. I am no longer looking for a punishing diet.

Lord, teach me to give food its proper place.

A man has joy by the answer of his mouth,
And a word spoken in due season, how good it is!
—Prov. 15:23

I am amazed when I think of how God has used little things that people have said to give me hope. There have been times when I was at the end of my rope and a friend would "just happen" to call to check on me.

I found Remuda Ranch through a friend who knew a lady who worked there. It gives me peace to know that God can use people and circumstances to make sure my needs get met.

Today, I am struggling with my relationship with my husband. We have a way of bringing out the worst in each other, and at times the marriage doesn't seem worth all the pain.

In the middle of all my confusion and doubt, I talked to a woman who is in the process of getting a divorce. She had no idea what I was dealing with, but through her sharing, I now have hope about my marriage.

There have been times in my recovery that I have been close to slipping. I knew that I was in danger, but would not take steps to keep myself safe. In the nick of time, I received a call or a card from someone who loved me. It was enough to keep me going.

Thank you, Lord, for providing me with hope.

Joseph said to them, "Do not be afraid, for am I in the place of God? But as for you, you meant evil against me; but God meant it for good, in order to bring it about as it is this day, to save many people alive."
—Gen. 50:19–20

It wasn't long ago that I surveyed the ruins of my life and decided to let God remake me in his mold. I am in the middle of God's remodeling process right now, and I often want to jump out of the mold. The desire for a quick fix for my abuse and suffering is constant. I want to be fixed instantly, but the Lord wants to remake me and conform me to the image of his Son. Why is it such a painful process?

Joseph was a product of God's remodeling. He suffered abandonment, slavery, imprisonment, betrayal, and more. His brothers meant to harm him, but God used it for good. God used these heartaches to forge a beautiful character in Joseph. He was full of compassion, patience, and understanding for others.

Can I trust God to do this same good work with my heartaches? "God is faithful, by whom you were called into the fellowship of His Son, Jesus Christ our Lord" (1 Cor. 1:9).

It is time for me to start acting like a product of his remodeling factory, rather than the boss of it. I choose to trust my Lord. He suffered the ultimate in abuse and abandonment for my sake.

———

Lord, you do know my pain. When I dread being in your mold, remind me that I can trust you.

> *For if the blood of bulls and goats and the ashes of*
> *a heifer, sprinkling the unclean, sanctifies for the*
> *purifying of the flesh, how much more shall the*
> *blood of Christ, who through the eternal Spirit*
> *offered Himself without spot to God, cleanse*
> *your conscience from dead works to serve the*
> *living God?*
> —Heb. 9:13–14

As I faced myself in treatment, I became over-whelmed with guilt for all the rotten things I had done in my life. My guilt and shame paralyzed me and kept me from progressing. I knew that Christ had died for my sins, but I was unwilling to accept his forgiveness.

One of the therapists put me through an exercise that helped me visualize being freed from my sins and guilt. She had spray-painted a huge rock white. I was instructed to write all of my sins on the rock with a marker.

After I had done that, I was asked to walk around carrying the rock. It was so heavy and bulky; it was hard for me to make much progress with that huge burden. After I had lugged it around for a while, the therapist told me to put it in a box, cover it with a lid, and then carry the whole thing for some time.

When I told her I was ready to let go and stop carrying my own burden of sin, we walked to a place where a cross stood. I buried all my sins at the foot of the cross and left them there.

Father, when I start dwelling on the sins of my past, remind me that I left them at the foot of the cross.

*Set your mind on things above, not on things on
the earth.*
—Col. 3:2

My friend Robert always says, "So what?" when I'm
in the middle of some huge emotional crisis. He is not
trying to make my feelings seem insignificant; instead,
he is trying to help me put things in perspective!

When I allow myself to wallow in the problems I am
facing, it is easy to let my fears control me. I spend so
much time thinking about what might happen that I
paralyze my thinking.

The pain I am facing today is very real; there's no
denying that I am in serious trouble. Yet I have felt like
this before, and I lived through it!

When I look at the big picture, I know I will get
through this pain just as I have done before. I am trying
to look at things as God might. What ugliness can be
shaved off me as I endure this pain? Is it possible that I
will be stronger on the other side of this mess? What
lessons can I learn while I am in this process? Maybe
I'll be equipped to help another hurting soul through
my struggles.

It's not easy, but I am trying to keep a heavenly perspective while I plow through this earthly muck. It
really helps.

_____

*Lord, remind me that this is not all there is to life; I have the hope of
better things to come!*

> *She shall be called Woman.*
> —Gen. 2:23

I was a Superwoman, always on the go, doing, doing, doing. I knew I was wearing myself out, but I couldn't stop. Everything seemed urgent and important. I couldn't even take time to sort out my priorities. My inner life was nonexistent except for my compulsions, and my garden of growth was dying.

I had become so absorbed in activity that I lost myself. I was obsessed with achievement, but it was never enough. I had to do more and more to gain a sense of identity. Compulsive exercise filled my days and I never relaxed. I received praise for my appearance and for how much I could accomplish. Inside I felt acceptable, even superior to others.

Real relationships were impossible for me! That involved just being a person, and I was unable to master that. I had lost the positive aspects of my femininity: sensitivity, discernment, the ability to nurture and encourage others.

One definition of recovery is "to find that which is lost." I had lost my womanhood, and I realized that femininity is more about "being" than "doing." Learning to say no meant admitting that I was no Superwoman. I asked God to replant my inner garden, and I did my part to help it grow. I stopped believing that I was worthless unless I was perfect.

Lord, thank you for the privilege of being a woman.

And the complacency of fools will destroy them.
—Prov. 1:32

I practiced my eating disorder for thirteen years; that was almost half of my lifetime! Many years of my life were consumed with pain because I chose to believe that the problem was less serious than it actually was.

During the first stages of anorexia I was thrilled with the weight loss. I gained attention for my new appearance and I was elated! I did not know that I was starting down a path that would eventually end near death.

When my parents realized that I was not eating, they forced me to eat. I complied, but decided not to keep the food down. At that point in my disease, I still thought I was just afraid of getting fat; I did not realize that there were secrets buried in my heart.

After I got married, my husband requested that I stop throwing up; he thought it was wasteful. Compliant to a fault, I stopped throwing up! But I was unable to stop eating compulsively. There was too much pain in my life, and I did not know how else to deal with it. It was not until I became depressed and suicidal that I knew I had to get help.

Lord, thank you for saving me from my complacency.

Rise up, my love, my fair one,
And come away.
For lo, the winter is past,
The rain is over and gone.
The flowers appear on the earth;
The time of singing has come,
And the voice of the turtledove
Is heard in our land.

—Song 2:10–12

The winter before I entered treatment for my eating disorder, there were no flowers. The birds had ceased their singing; there were only brittle sounds of silence. The winter was cold, the rains dark and depressing. I thought my face and body looked fat and ugly. I felt that God had surely forsaken me; he had turned his eyes from me.

My disease had taken me to the bottom of a dark pit. There was no hope, no love, no laughter, no joy. Then it was as if Jesus said to me, "This is enough. The winter is past; it's time to live. Come, my fair one, come with me and I'll show you the way. The way is through me, and I will be with you at all times."

The way was not easy. Entering treatment was scary and facing life without the buffer of food was painful. For the first time in my life, though, I can really see and smell the flowers! I can appreciate their beauty and their sweet fragrance. I can hear the birds singing and I enjoy their sweet songs. I now see myself as Jesus does, as lovely and lovable.

Father, thank you for bringing me through the winter.

*Now, therefore, you are no longer strangers and
foreigners, but fellow citizens with the saints and
members of the household of God.*

—Eph. 2:19

Many times I felt like I didn't belong; I felt excluded
and separated from people. My self-esteem was so low
that I did not feel worthy of being part of a group. I
could be among crowds and still feel alone!

Now I realize that I alienated myself from others. I
did not connect to people because I feared they would
reject me. Keeping my distance in relationships allowed me to feel safe, though it also provided lots of
loneliness.

I used my eating disorder to shelter me from the real
world. I could tell myself that even if I felt left out, food
was always there for me.

Food is not much of a companion! It's hard to become intimate with a hamburger and fries. Even when
I filled my stomach with food, my heart was still empty
and aching.

Since I became part of God's family, I feel less alone!
I don't feel like such a stranger anymore. Having God
in my life has given me the strength to take risks with
people. I am learning to be confident because I know
he loves me, no matter what!

*Lord, I ask that you give me the courage to take part in life. Give me
the confidence that I lack.*

> *If I say, "My foot slips,"*
> *Your mercy, O LORD, will hold me up.*
> *In the multitude of my anxieties within me,*
> *Your comforts delight my soul.*
>
> —Ps. 94:18–19

The last three months have been full of many changes. I have moved to a new city, started a new job, and begun to meet new people. I live in a new home, attend a new church, and have to deal with new financial pressures.

Impulsively, I ate, ate, ate to regain some control, and soon I returned to old bulimic patterns. I was sinking fast, and I refused to believe that my disease could take over again. For three weeks I denied that I was in relapse.

Finally, scared out of my mind, I entered the bathroom. I got down on my knees, not to purge, but to cry out to God. I said, "God, you know the battle I am faced with; I'm slipping fast! You know that Satan wants to defeat me and drag me down into the pit. I need your power and might to defeat this; I can't do it alone."

The impulse is still there, but because of my prayers that day, it isn't as strong. Each time I enter a bathroom, particularly after a meal, I remember that day on my knees before God. He now enters with me; I'm not alone!

Lord, thank you for holding me up when I slip.

Unless the LORD had been my help,
My soul would soon have settled in silence.
—Ps. 94:17

I am amazed when I look back at the events of my life! My history is full of pain that could have had devastating results.

The things that have happened to me have not been easy to face. I am in agony as I recall childhood memories. Secrets are buried so deeply in my mind, I sometimes wonder if I'll ever stop uncovering new ones.

When I look at all the pain in my life, it amazes me that I lived through it. What kept me from curling up and dying? The only answer I know is God.

If God had not been with me when I was raped and incested and molested as a child, how could I have survived? If he had not given me the strength to get help for my eating disorder, I would not have made it!

God was with me while I was in treatment at Remuda Ranch. Conquering my eating disorder would have been impossible without his power working in me.

Today God is with me as I am separated from my husband. He is near as I agonize over the decisions that must be made.

I don't think I could have survived the pain of life without him!

Father, I thank you for preserving me from myself and all my enemies.

So, if you think you are standing firm, be careful that you don't fall!
—1 Cor. 10:12 NIV

My life seemed perfect. We had found our dream home, a great new church, and I loved my new job. My recovery from anorexia and bulimia was going well. I had even taken on the responsibility of leading a Bible study with an emphasis on problems with food and eating. I was feeling pretty smug about things.

Then it happened! I just couldn't stand being content. Was I so used to turmoil that I set out to create a crisis? Suddenly, the house needed so much; there were strangers at church; my job became overwhelming.

All these pressures led to a return to my eating disorder. Now how could I possibly lead a Bible study while I was in relapse?

Before I moved, quit my job, stopped going to church, and declined to lead the Bible study, God helped me see what was going on. He gave me the strength to retrace the solid, familiar steps of recovery. I found stability in praying, journaling, returning to support groups, and following my food plan.

Lord, forgive me for my pridefulness. Thank you for reminding me what I need to do to keep from falling again.

"And whoever will not receive you nor hear your words, when you depart from that house or city, shake off the dust from your feet."
—Matt. 10:14

I'm always disappointed when my expectations are not met. Mind you, these are not just any expectations. They are mine, and I'm a perfectionist. My ideals are pretty high.

Recovery seems simple enough to me. I'll explain my situation and share my pain. Then people will understand me; maybe they'll even comfort me and be properly sympathetic.

The problem is, people don't always do what I want. I've learned that doing what's right does not guarantee supportive responses from those around me. My friend says, "They just don't get it!" It's especially painful when it happens with people who I think should be understanding.

I've decided that it is not my job to educate the entire world on the dangers of eating disorders. Nor can I expect all those around me to agree with me or support me in my plan of recovery. It is important that I am doing what God wants me to do. This enables me to say my piece and go away knowing that I have done my part.

God, help me learn to rely on your acceptance of me.

> *How long, O you sons of men,*
> *Will you turn my glory to shame?*
> *How long will you love worthlessness*
> *And seek falsehood?*
> *But know that the LORD has set apart*
>   *for Himself him who is godly;*
> *The LORD will hear when I call to Him.*
> —Ps. 4:2–3

When I was in treatment for anorexia I got up early each morning to read and study my Bible. As I studied the fourth Psalm one morning, I learned who I really am.

Sometimes verses don't seem to apply to my situation, but this passage really caught my eye. In verse 2, I substituted "anorectics/bulimics" for "sons of men." I realized the worthlessness I loved and the falsehoods I sought were body image, weight, and food.

God showed me that I was his glory but that I was spoiling it. He thought enough of me to set me apart for himself!

I did not want to turn God's glory into shame, so I called out to him and he truly heard me. From that day on, I have tried to remember who God tells me I am, instead of the lies I have been telling myself.

Lord Jesus, hear me now! I no longer want to turn your glory into shame.

WALK WITH ME

I see your face
and feel your pain,
the tear on your cheek, your cloak
   of shame.

I reach out My hand
and ask you to walk and
talk a while.

I am your Lord;
I will not give you more burdens
than you can bear.

Just walk with Me and
talk with Me. My
love I will share.

The path you take
is raft with despair.

Just walk with Me and
talk with Me; I will
shower you with care.

Lay down your cloak of shame,
give to Me your burdens of pain.

Just walk with Me and
talk with Me.
I am your Lord and
I will restore you to life again.

*For what I am doing, I do not understand. For
what I will to do, that I do not practice; but what
I hate, that I do.*   —Rom. 7:15

I find such hope in Paul's writing. This man knows
what it feels like to be powerless. He says it so well! I
can really relate to what I hear him saying: "Man, I
know what I want to do, but I can't seem to make myself do it!"

My faulty thinking has been perfected over the
years with lots of practice. The process of changing my
thoughts is tedious, frustrating, and sometimes overwhelming.

Wearing masks to please others and numbing my
feelings with food were effective survival techniques
for a while. Unfortunately, not only did I numb myself
to pain, but to the joy around me!

I no longer need those coping tools. I have learned
new ways of dealing with life, but I still find it hard to
react differently! The disease that crippled me emotionally is not easy to let go!

I remind myself that this recovery process is just
that—a process. It took me years of practice to hone
the unhealthy skills, and it will take time to make
changes. I am learning to forgive myself for my imperfections. With God's help I am getting well!

Father, I see your strength through my powerlessness!

For we are to God the fragrance of Christ among those who are being saved and among those who are perishing.   —2 Cor. 2:15

Smells have a powerful effect on me! I can get a whiff of something and be hurtled ten years into the past. My memories are often triggered by odors of which I have no conscious recollection.

My Aunt Teri's house always smells like bacon and coffee. When I'm around that aroma I feel warm and safe, because my aunt had a way of making me feel that way.

One of my good friends wears a fragrance that I often smell on other people. Each time I smell it I think of special times we shared and how much that friendship means to me. My friend connects that scent with good memories.

There are other odors that I try to avoid. Some things trigger painful memories that I have tried hard to forget. For example, because of a childhood experience the smell of newsprint makes me nauseated. I have trouble even reading the newspaper because I have such a powerful physical response to that odor.

I am glad to know that God thinks of me as "the fragrance of Christ," that when he smells me, he smells Jesus.

Father, I am so grateful that you do not smell my rotting heart, but only smell the fragrance of Jesus.

> *My son, give attention to my words;*
> *Incline your ear to my sayings.*
> *Do not let them depart from your eyes;*
> *Keep them in the midst of your heart;*
> *For they are life to those who find them,*
> *And health to all their flesh.*
>
> —Prov. 4:20–22

Dealing with my stubborn four-year-old is like looking into a mirror, and it's not a pretty sight! No matter what I ask of him, he usually responds, "I don't want to!" Trying to convince him that I know what's best is useless. He is determined to ignore my instruction and will have to suffer the consequences.

Sadly, I often respond to God the same way. Whether he is gently encouraging me to step out in faith or clearly directing me through his Word, I repeatedly choose not to listen. Like the children of Israel, I find myself going around the mountain one more time.

I don't believe that it is God's plan for me to struggle this way. My own fears and doubts keep me from experiencing his blessings. Refusing to trust what he says in his Word brings failure in my life. My mind becomes cluttered with human reasoning, so I am limited to my own ability. Doubt robs me of God's best for my life.

Today, I choose to pay attention to his words! I want health and life.

Father, thank you for giving me directions for life.

Then He commanded the multitudes to sit down on the grass. And He took the five loaves and the two fish, and looking up to heaven, He blessed and broke and gave the loaves to the disciples; and the disciples gave to the multitudes.

—Matt. 14:19

I believed that God was only available to me for the big problems of life. I didn't feel I could bother him with the daily struggles I faced. The God I grew up with was strict and punishing; often I was afraid to approach him.

As I began my healing process many issues felt overwhelming. Some days I struggled to eat each bite of food, and other times I was afraid I would eat everything in sight!

There have been days when food has not been an issue at all, but the situations around me were difficult to handle. Managing my recovery along with my responsibilities as a mother and wife has been extremely challenging! When I started a part-time job, my life became even fuller.

I read in the Bible that Jesus was concerned with all the needs of people. Although his main focus was on the condition of hearts, he did not neglect to tend to the physical needs of the body.

At times I have felt guilty for taking time out to meet my physical needs. It is comforting to remember that God created all of me; each aspect of my life is important to him.

Lord, I'm glad that all my needs are important to you.

The LORD will guide you always;
he will satisfy your needs in a sun-scorched land
and will strengthen your frame.
You will be like a well-watered garden,
like a spring whose waters never fail.

—Isa. 58:11 NIV

Sitting in chapel one day during my treatment at Remuda Ranch, I was overwhelmed by the impact of where I was. The tears flowed and, though I was surrounded by other residents and staff, I felt alone with God.

I pictured him standing at the gates of heaven with his arms outstretched. God was calling me back to him. My heart cried out to him, "I surrender; no longer can I waste away and run from you."

I read this verse on that day, and it spoke directly to my heart. The Lord had brought me from Alaska, where my life had become frozen and brittle, to the sun-scorched land of Arizona. He was satisfying my needs and watering the parched garden of my aching heart. In the middle of the desert God had begun to heal my mind, body, and spirit.

It has been over one year since that day. The struggles of recovery from my eating disorder have been many, but the victories have been precious!

Father, I thank you for allowing the healing to begin.

Bringing every thought into captivity to the
obedience of Christ.   —2 Cor. 10:5

I struggle with unhealthy thoughts, especially during my morning shower. I'm not sure why, but my fears get out of control as I start my day. The most insignificant thing can turn into "crazy-making" if I allow a tiny idea to take control of my mind.

One way I have found to combat this is to talk out loud to God. I feel safe asking God over the roar of the shower water to capture my thoughts.

Yesterday in the shower I started obsessing about a hurtful comment I made to someone who has been very supportive of me. I made a conscious effort to accept God's forgiveness for my unkind words, but the guilt persisted. I began audibly to ask for God's help in overcoming the paralyzing thoughts. I cried as I became overwhelmed with guilt about what I had done. Fear took over as I considered how I might be rejected for my ugliness.

The thoughts continued to plague me all morning. Finally I made a phone call to the person I had offended. I asked for forgiveness and accepted it.

I am learning to ask God to take my thoughts before they capture and destroy me.

Father, please purify my thoughts; keep me safe!

> *But why do you judge your brother? Or why do you show contempt for your brother? For we shall all stand before the judgment seat of Christ.*
>
> —Rom. 14:10

I allow some people to make me feel intimidated. I think they are prettier, or smarter, or have more money than I do. I think others have a better life than mine.

I worked with a woman who I thought had everything; I really felt inadequate around her. Once I let go of my insecurity and got to know her, I learned how wrong I was. This beautiful, "together" woman had grown up with great pain. Her father was an alcoholic, and her mother enabled him to stay sick through her own denial.

This woman grew up in a home that was not safe; she never knew how her dad would react when he came home from work. She chose early in life not to be like her father, so she got an education and made a clean break from her family. She went through therapy to deal with the pain in her past.

As our friendship grew I realized that we had much in common. Beneath her air of confidence were many of the same fears and insecurities that I had. She is now a great example to me because she has worked through much of her pain.

God, when I hide in my insecurity, I miss out on so much! Remind me that underneath the surface we are all pretty much the same.

But those who wait on the LORD
Shall renew their strength;
They shall mount up with wings like eagles,
They shall run and not be weary,
They shall walk and not faint.

—Isa. 40:31

It excites me to know that God gives me the capacity to soar like an eagle! He looks past my limitations and sees me as strong and free. My part in his vision is to learn to wait on him before I go jumping out of any nests!

One definition of waiting is to remain in expectation or readiness. Waiting involves yielding my own desires to the Lord. Many times my own desires are not suited to my real needs, but I find myself running ahead of God with my own plans. I must surrender my desires to God and ask him to show me what his plans are for me.

As yielding becomes my practice, I find renewed strength and freedom. Gradually I am able to withstand the temptation to abuse food. God has used my time of waiting to teach me many things. I am learning to deal with life in new ways, and I judge myself by performance less and less. There is real freedom in this new way of life!

Father, remind me that there is much to be gained in waiting on you.

> *What the chewing locust left, the*
> *swarming locust has eaten;*
> *What the swarming locust left, the*
> *crawling locust has eaten;*
> *And what the crawling locust left,*
> *the consuming locust has eaten. . . .*
> *So I will restore to you the years that*
> *the swarming locust has eaten,*
> *The crawling locust,*
> *The consuming locust,*
> *And the chewing locust.*
> —Joel 1:4; 2:25

So much of my life has been wasted! As a youngster I was fearful and insecure; I spent my time seeking approval and avoiding pain. My eating disorder emerged when I was fifteen. So almost half of my life was consumed with my obsession about my body and food.

The part of my life that was not consumed by the eating disorder was taken up by my unhealthy thinking. I was overly concerned about what others thought of me. I never felt like my contributions to life were acceptable; I always fell short of perfection.

In order to combat the feelings of unworthiness, I became compulsive in my behavior. I was always going and doing! The house was never clean enough; the cupboards were never full enough. At least that's what I thought.

I have often wished that my life was like a video tape; I longed to rewind it and make a new picture. God says that he will restore to me the years that were lost. I choose to cling to that hope.

Lord, please give me a new start at life!

MATURE UNDERSTANDING – *May 11*

Brethren, do not be children in understanding;
however, in malice be babes, but in understanding
be mature.
                                        —1 Cor. 14:20

My eight-year-old son came home from school last week bursting with news. He could hardly wait to tell me what had taken place that day! This is unusual for him, so I knew something interesting must have happened.

After we had gotten settled at home, he began. Through his blow-by-blow description I learned that his teacher had "faded" (fainted)! He went on to give his impression of the whole scene. I wondered how much of what he was saying was true and how much had been conjured up by his classmates.

It struck me that many of the memories that plague me today are from a child's perspective. The abuse that took place in my childhood is real, but I wonder how much of it has gotten blown out of proportion over the years. Abusing my body with food does not make my understanding any clearer!

There is also a part of me that would like to deny all the horrible memories I have. Through therapy I'm trying to bring mature understanding to those memories. Doing that is painful, but it is another step in my healing.

Lord, please help me understand the pain!

May 12 – TAKE HEED!

*Therefore let him who thinks he stands
take heed lest he fall.*

—1 Cor. 10:12

Recently I got stuck in traffic. At first I couldn't figure out what the delay was, but then I saw the problem. A man was driving a truck with a camper on it, and the camper door was swinging wide open! Drivers all around slowed down to honk and point to the danger. People attempted to warn the man of his unsafe condition.

I made an effort to get the driver's attention by waving, but he just nodded and smiled. I got the impression that he knew the door was open. I assumed that either he didn't care, or there was a factor unknown to me that made him comfortable with the situation.

I could not help thinking about the parallel between that traffic jam and my life. As I progressed in my eating disorder, there were many warnings along the way that I chose to ignore.

People remarked about my varying weight and I could always come up with an excuse for it. Though I had many tests done because of my awful stomach problems, the doctors seemed mystified as to the source. Dentists commented on the poor condition of my teeth and gums, but I chose to deny that my eating disorder was a serious threat to my health.

Are there warning signals in your life that you are choosing to ignore? Pay attention before it's too late!

Lord, thank you for saving my life.

"I will be a Father to you,
And you shall be My sons and daughters,
Says the LORD Almighty."
—2 Cor. 6:18

Few of the women I know have a healthy view of their fathers. Dads of this world are often distant or aloof, and some are absent altogether. Some fathers struggle with alcoholism and fits of anger. As men, dads often have a hard time relating to daughters.

As a little girl, I thought my daddy was godlike. He could do no wrong, and my only desire was to please him. There is still a part of that little girl in the grown woman I have become. I still find myself doing things in hopes of gaining my father's acceptance.

My biggest struggle lies in viewing God in the same way I view my earthly father. I have transferred many of the hurts and disappointments I experienced with my dad to my heavenly Father. I wonder how God will take care of my needs when my dad could not do it adequately.

I am thankful for this verse that tells me that God really is my Father, and I am his daughter. I continue to work on separating my memories of my dad from the way I view God.

Thank you, Father, for calling me your daughter. Help me learn to trust you.

When He rose up from prayer, and had come to
His disciples, He found them sleeping from sorrow.
—Luke 22:45

Lately the events in my life have taken some scary turns. I made some choices that have had painful consequences, and I have had to deal with the sorrow of my lost dreams. I worried that I would be unable to sleep because I was so tense, but I have been blessed with a full night's rest even in the midst of my pain.

Before I entered treatment for my eating disorder my life was full of pain. I could hardly motivate myself to do even the most simple tasks. I slept many hours away, trying to forget the pain of life.

Once the healing process began, there were times when I slept out of depression. At times the emotional strain was so great that my body just needed time to rest.

I no longer have to sleep my life away; God is doing wonderful things in my life. Yet I am grateful for the hours of rest when my mind and body can take a break from thinking and feeling.

Lord, I thank you for the ability to rest. I give you the sorrow in my heart.

"Yes, and why, even of yourselves, do you not judge what is right?"
—Luke 12:57

My inner voice usually tells me what is right and wrong, but I have trained myself to mistrust all my thoughts and feelings. I do not believe that I should live only by what my feelings say, though they are a part of me and are often accurate.

I often look to others for answers to questions that I already have! And it's not enough to hear that one person agrees with me; I tend to survey all those whose opinions I respect.

That method of making choices really has some drawbacks! One problem is that it is not possible to get everyone I ask to agree on one answer. I also find it frustrating to do something that goes against what I want to do.

I have decided that the only way to make choices is to weigh my options, ask for advice if I really want it, pray for wisdom, and then take a chance! In this way I am taking responsibility for myself.

I am learning to trust my intuition. I am not always wrong! Many times that still, small voice inside knew the answer all along.

Father, thank you for giving me wisdom to know what is right for me.

*What purpose then does the law serve? It was
added because of transgressions.* —Gal. 3:19

On a recent trip, I rounded a curve while exceeding
the speed limit. A policeman passed me driving the
opposite direction. He turned his headlights on, leaned
forward in his seat, and pointed his finger directly at
me! His actions reminded me that I was not obeying
the law. I was breaking the rules of the road, and I
needed to be reminded that there are consequences
for that.

For the remainder of my trip, I was very conscious of
my speed. Having been confronted with what I was
doing wrong made me aware of my behavior for some
time.

The following day I again exceeded the speed limit.
It was as if I had no fear of wrongdoing. In only one day
I had forgotten my confrontation with the law.

There are rules to follow for my recovery. I have a
food plan to live by, and there is definitely a cost to be
paid if I fail to adhere to it. Sometimes it takes being
confronted with the cost before I am willing to follow
the rules. My body can't function forever if I keep abusing it.

Lord, help me be willing to follow the rules.

GOD DON'T MAKE NO JUNK! – *May 17*

> *My frame was not hidden from*
>   *You,*
> *When I was made in secret,*
> *And skillfully wrought in the lowest*
>   *parts of the earth.*
> —Ps. 139:15

I was skillfully wrought? You must be kidding! You mean God planned for me to look like this?" Many times when I look in the mirror, these thoughts pass through my head.

Before recovery I hated my body and everything about me. Truthfully, I hated God for making me look the way I did. I despised what he had wrought, and I spent time, energy, and money trying to recreate myself. I was willing to sacrifice everything in my quest for a perfect body.

It has been a struggle to accept my body. There have been times when I've ignored everything below my neck. I avoided looking in the mirror because the self-hatred was so intense.

I am now coming to terms with the fact that God made me with loving hands. He gave me this body; he didn't just throw me together! God fashioned me; that implies that he took time and thought about what he was going to make. I am the result of a project that took God time and effort. He cared about what he made, and he still does!

Dearest Lord, help me to grow to accept and love what you have made.

> *Have I not commanded you? Be strong and of good courage; do not be afraid, nor be dismayed, for the LORD your God is with you wherever you go.*
>
> —Josh. 1:9

This verse has become one of my favorites! Many times in the past few years I have remembered this promise from God. When I feel weak and lonely, I am often reminded that God is actually with me. Even when my eating disorder threatens to take over, he is there!

It is so hard to be strong and courageous. Much of the time I am terrified by the things I face. Sometimes even things like eating a meal, taking a test, or seeing a friend seem overwhelming! But doing things becomes easier when I remember that God is there for me.

With his strength, I have been able to do things that I would have never considered doing without God. He gave me the courage to face my eating disorder, enter treatment, and uncover many painful memories that were locked deep inside me.

God is with me and I know he is with you! Turn to him for the strength and courage that you need to face your day. Don't be afraid.

———————

Lord, help me remember that things are not so terrifying when I look to you for courage.

And let us not grow weary while doing good, for in due season we shall reap if we do not lose heart.
—Gal. 6:9

It is so easy to want to quit; giving up sometimes seems like the answer. I am doing what I think is right, following the plan that was suggested for my recovery. I just want to see the results more quickly! I am so used to gratifying my needs instantly that it is very difficult to wait.

During treatment for my eating disorder I worked on a plan of recovery that would achieve the desired results. It includes going to support groups weekly, seeing my therapist, and dealing with the issues that are giving me trouble. Following a food plan that the nutritionist prescribed is also part of the picture.

I am doing my best to follow the program, but the results are slow in coming. I do see changes in my life; there are things in me that are new and different. My biggest problem is being patient while the process is taking place.

I get tired of doing all that it takes to stay healthy, but the alternatives are not too bright. I recall vividly how unhealthy I was before recovery. That helps me keep going when I feel like quitting. I choose not to give up the fight; I know my time will come!

Lord, give me the strength to keep doing what is needed to stay healthy.

This is the day the LORD has made;
We will rejoice and be glad in it.
—Ps. 118:24

Life is not fair; why me, Lord?" Many times I've fallen into the trap of feeling sorry for myself. It is easy to wallow in self-pity and make excuses for my attitude.

Strength comes when I am not afraid to face each day, no matter what is in store for me. I remind myself daily that God will not give me more burdens than I can bear (1 Cor. 10:13).

Peace comes to me when I live each day as it comes, not agonizing over yesterday or fearing tomorrow. I struggle to praise the Lord for the day he has given me. It is hard to stay in the moment; I find myself dwelling in the past or projecting what the future may bring.

With the Lord's help, I can praise him for this new day. He will help me let go of yesterday and not obsess about tomorrow.

Dear Lord, I praise you for the day you have made. Remind me that you will not give me more than I can bear today.

And Jesus said to them, "I am the bread of life. He who comes to Me shall never hunger, and he who believes in Me shall never thirst." —John 6:35

During the time that I was controlled by bulimia I never seemed to get full. I had stretched my stomach to such a capacity that I never felt physically satisfied. Although I ate inordinate amounts of food, I still felt empty.

When I was required to eat in front of other people, I always ate before the designated meal. I was so out of touch with what a normal portion of food was that I tried to fill myself up so I would not overeat around others.

My food was never processed in my body in a normal manner, so I was terrified if I could not get rid of a meal right away. My life was completely out of control.

Since I underwent treatment for my eating disorder my body has begun to function more normally. I have been amazed to learn that my body is able to process meals in the way it was designed. Although I am not eating huge quantities any longer, I actually feel full!

I have learned that much of my hunger came from the pain and emptiness of my soul. Through a relationship with Jesus, I'm getting full on the inside, too!

Lord, make me aware when my hunger is not physical.

If indeed you have heard Him and have been taught by Him, as the truth is in Jesus: that you put off, concerning your former conduct, the old man which grows corrupt according to the deceitful lusts, and be renewed in the spirit of your mind, and that you put on the new man which was created according to God, in true righteousness and holiness.
　　　　　　　　　　　　　—Eph. 4:21–24

As I recover I search for my true identity. Who am I? What does it mean to be me? I find myself acting quiet and considerate, gentle and caring. I am becoming honest and more aware of things around me.

I have always envied quiet people. I used to be loud and wild; it was a way to cover up the pain inside me. I realize that I am now the person I longed to be!

It is not necessary for me to hide anymore. Having someone disapprove of me does not destroy me now; I am growing secure in God's love and acceptance.

When I learned that this new me is valuable with or without the approval of others, a huge burden was lifted. I am now free to be who God made me to be.

God is remaking me into the being he planned for me to be. I am becoming new in him.

Father, thank you for the new person I am becoming.

Oh, taste and see that the LORD is good;
Blessed is the man who trusts in Him!
          —Ps. 34:8

My life was based on fear and guilt and shame for twenty-eight years! Because of that the spiritual perspective that I grew up with seemed harsh and unloving. I felt so judged and condemned that I built thick walls around my heart. I wouldn't even trust God not to judge me.

I sometimes wonder if I will ever be able to trust anyone, even God. My trust has been violated so many times that I assume everyone wants to hurt me. It is hard for me to accept things at face value.

Looking back, I realize that I closed my heart to God a long time ago. I decided as a child that if so-called "responsible" adults were not worthy of my trust, then God was unreliable as well. I spent years of my life angry at him. That in turn gave me even more guilt!

Acting out with food was the only way I knew to relieve myself of the guilt and anger. It didn't work very well, but my eating disorder did distract me from some of the pain in my life.

I am now taking a new look at God, but it is hard to separate him from the one I knew as a child. I admit that I am finding him good and faithful, not at all like I thought he would be!

Father, please be gentle with my tender heart.

> *By your endurance you will gain your lives.*
> —Luke 21:19 RSV

I have watched as a baby chick starts to break out of the shell. The bird is weak and frail, but slowly and methodically it pecks away at the hard substance that surrounds it.

The chick has to rest often and gather strength to continue the job. The baby bird does not give up, because there is no life on the inside of that shell. Unless the bird endures the struggle and frees itself, it will die without ever seeing life on the outside.

I have struggled to resist helping the baby bird. It would be so easy for me to peel away the shell and free the chick all at once. That would not really be a help, though. Without the effort of cracking the shell and crawling out, the bird would not become strong enough to live on the outside.

Becoming free of this eating disorder is much like the bird getting free of its shell. I know God could free me from the bondage all at one time; it would be easy for him! But God knows what is best for me, and he is aware that I am gaining strength by daily pecking away at little pieces of the hard wall around me.

Even while that chick is confined to its shell, changes and growth are taking place. I am not whole today, but I am on my way!

God, give me the strength I need to endure!

God is our refuge and strength,
A very present help in trouble.
Therefore we will not fear,
Even though the earth be removed,
And though the mountains be carried into the
*   midst of the sea;*
Though its waters roar and be troubled,
Though the mountains shake with its swelling.
—Ps. 46:1–3

God, what's wrong with me? Why am I not able to rely on you for my strength? I want to trust you, really I do, but I am afraid to talk to you for fear of what will happen. I keep thinking you're going to be angry at me like my dad.

I don't want to feel stupid for making mistakes, Lord. I'd like to think I could tell you anything, even the deep, dark secrets in my heart. What keeps me from sharing with you? After all, you already know my thoughts. I am only fooling myself to think that I can hide from you.

I struggle to find my refuge in you. Some pretty scary stuff has happened in my lifetime! Does being sexually abused count? This eating disorder sure feels like it's going to be the end of me. Having a child with special needs seems like a disaster to me.

There is no refuge if it's not you! I can't find the strength I need in myself, and food is certainly no help. Money is hard to count on, and the perfect body I desire seems out of reach. I'm in big trouble!

God, please teach me how to rely on you.

Rest in the LORD, and wait patiently for Him.
—Ps. 37:7

Just as I did not become bulimic overnight, recovery did not take place instantly. For me the process of healing took several years.

There were periods when I experienced a recurrence of my symptoms. I reverted to bingeing and purging when my life seemed out of control or when I was dealing with tough issues. Slipping into old behaviors was discouraging and often caused me to question whether or not I was really recovering.

I want to dictate the terms of my recovery! I know what my issues are; now I want immediate resolution of them so I can get on with my life.

I am thankful for the Lord's perfect wisdom. He knows just how much I can handle at one time. I want instant healing, much like instant potatoes. He wants my recovery to be the real thing, not the freeze-dried variety.

The Lord knows that I can't deal with intense issues constantly. Sometimes I need to rest and enjoy the fruits of my labor. He knows when I'm ready to move to a new level of wholeness.

Lord, teach me to wait patiently for you.

Their soul abhorred all manner of food,
And they drew near to the gates of death.
Then they cried out to the LORD in their trouble,
And He saved them out of their distresses.
—Ps. 107:18–19

When my teenage daughter got braces her mouth hurt so badly that she could not even eat. She cried and cried; she hated those braces!

I hurt for her and wanted desperately to take her pain away. I knew that while that wasn't possible, I could help her. At the store I picked out soft food, pudding, and soup to help her through the rough time.

I know God wants to help me. Sometimes I get so discouraged that I hate life itself and believe I can't possibly go on. It breaks God's heart to see his child suffer so. He wants so much to hear me cry out to him for help, and he is always willing and ready to rescue me!

As an anorectic, I hated food. I did draw near the gates of death, more than once. But when I cried out to my Father, he fed me the soft food of his love to restore me to spiritual and physical health.

Lord Jesus, hear my cry and save me!

> *I waited patiently for the LORD;*
> *And He inclined to me,*
> *And heard my cry.*
> *He also brought me up out of a horrible pit,*
> *Out of the miry clay,*
> *And set my feet upon a rock,*
> *And established my steps.*
> *He has put a new song in my mouth.*
>   —Ps. 40:1–3a

I was deep in depression and nothing seemed to help. Finally I made up my mind to wait on the Lord, mainly because I ran out of energy and gave up. I found that God is faithful to do what he promises when I let him work in my life.

During my treatment for anorexia, I learned that even in the midst of emotional pain, my feet can be planted firmly on the Rock. I made a choice to stop fighting God and wait on him. He not only lifted me up, but he also filled me with the joy of music again!

After having hardly touched a piano for fifteen years, I found myself drawn to the one in the dayroom at Remuda Ranch. I couldn't stay away; I played and sang every spare minute I had. In more ways than one, God put a new song in my mouth and my heart! It was worth waiting on him.

Thank you, Father, for the gifts that come from waiting on you.

Cause me to hear Your lovingkindness in the morning,
For in You do I trust;
Cause me to know the way in which I should walk,
For I lift up my soul to You.   —Ps. 143:8

There have been so many times in my life that I did not know which way to turn! I make myself crazy trying to decide exactly what to do. If I choose to allow them to, the choices in my life will swamp me.

What job is best suited for me? Do I need to go back to school? Is the amount I'm being paid enough? Should I take a new job?

Am I thin enough? What should I eat today? Can I trust what the professionals are telling me about my health? Do I really need to enter treatment for my eating disorder?

How will we ever afford children? Should I quit work and stay home with my baby? Are my parenting skills adequate? Will my kids be safe away from me?

Life is full of questions and decisions, and I often feel inadequate to do what is best. Since I have trusted God with my life, I know he will give me direction in making choices. It helps so much to give myself to him each day and ask him for wisdom and guidance.

Lord, I believe that you know which way is best for me. Please give me a push in that direction.

Why do You stand afar off, O LORD?
Why do You hide Yourself in times of trouble?
—Ps. 10:1

I love reading David's words in the book of Psalms! He is very open and honest with God. I could hear him paraphrasing Psalm 10:1 in today's jargon like this: "Hey, God, where are you when I need you?"

It does not seem natural to show anger toward God! Somehow I think if I don't verbalize my feelings, God won't know that I am unhappy about the way things are going. It just isn't so; he knows my heart.

David did some pretty rotten things in his lifetime, but he is considered "a man after [God's] heart" (Acts 13:22). Throughout the book of Psalms David pours out his heart to God; he is not afraid to share his true feelings with him.

I'm taking a step toward wholeness by being honest. I am determined to tell the truth, even if it hurts. This applies to God as well as others. God is all ears! I have found that he keeps my secrets even better than my most trusted friend.

I am learning to tell God everything. He doesn't mind when I whine and moan about the way my body looks; he'll comfort me when I want to eat everything in sight. Are you listening, God?

Father, thank you for listening to me.

A good name is better than precious ointment.
—Eccl. 7:1

The origin of my name has a painful memory connected to it. I love the name itself, but I have struggled to erase the shameful connotation it carries.

One day when I was in treatment for my eating disorder at Remuda Ranch, a gentleman visited in chapel. He spoke on the true meaning of an individual's name. He presented us each with a name tag, beautifully inscribed with our names and the biblical meanings underneath them.

I never saw that man again, but God used him to profoundly change how I view myself. Instead of associating my name with an ugly, shameful picture, I am now able to think of a positive, loving image.

When I told my parents how bad I felt about my name, they were astonished. They explained that they had spent hours trying to decide which name sounded the most beautiful for their first child.

As a little girl I did not pick up on that part of the story. Today I am learning to believe what God says about me. He lovingly calls me his child, and my name is precious to me.

Father, thank you for calling me your own. I value that name above all others.

HE GIVES LIFE!

Thank you, Lord, for giving me life; your grace has changed me forever!

You freely gave me wings when my parents were unable to give me the courage to fly.

Wings strong enough to soar to unknown places, where you continue to love and nurture my new life.

Each time my wings become weak, you hold me in your arms until my spirit is once again ready to trust you.

As I fly, the sunlight peers through the clouds in the midst of the rain.

It gathers together those who have faith to believe in the gifts it offers:

Encouragement, richness of character, and a better understanding of who we are.

God, I sense you gently nudging my soul to reveal the secret rainbow that awaits, as I endure.

> *Little children, keep yourselves from idols.*
> —1 John 5:21

When I think of the sin of idolatry, I think of golden statues. Can't you just picture the crowd of heathens bowing down to some useless piece of metal?

My idols don't come in gold, but they come in all sorts of other forms. I have made gods of people; although I don't actually bow down and worship them, I make their opinion of me more valuable than gold.

Food is another god in my life. I am now working on not eating too much or too little of it. But I still find myself feeling very insecure if there is too little food in the pantry.

A perfect body is something that I have said I would die for. Truthfully, many women do die striving to become perfect on the outside. I put far too much emphasis on my outward appearance.

God's Word says, "You shall have no other gods before Me" (Ex. 20:3). I sense him standing by, watching as all my other gods crumble around me. People disappoint me; their opinions can't always be trusted. Food was made just to fuel my body; it cannot give me security. Even a "perfect" body is no guarantee against life's pain. God is the only one worthy of my praise and adoration.

Father, forgive me for having other gods.

Can a woman forget her nursing child,
And not have compassion on the son of her womb?
Surely they may forget,
Yet I will not forget you.
See, I have inscribed you on the palms of My hands;
Your walls are continually before Me.

—Isa. 49:15–16

Earthly parents come in all varieties: good, loving, permissive, neglectful, and indifferent. No parent is perfect! You may have been blessed with wonderful, caring parents, or maybe you were rejected and neglected.

In any case, take comfort in the fact that God's Word promises that he will never forget you or stop loving you! I find such peace in that knowledge.

Many times I remind myself of something important. Writing notes or tying a string around my finger helps. I even have calendars on which I write important events—anything to jog my memory!

The nail prints in Christ's hands spell out your name; they serve to remind him of you. You're a special child of God and he loves you dearly! Even if others forget you or mistreat you, remember that you are important to God.

———————

Lord, thank you for the reminder that you will not forget me. I have spelled your name on my heart.

> *Therefore take up the whole armor of God, that*
> *you may be able to withstand in the evil day, and*
> *having done all to stand. Stand therefore, having*
> *girded your waist with truth, having put on the*
> *breastplate of righteousness, and having shod your*
> *feet with the preparation of the gospel of peace;*
> *above all, taking the shield of faith with which you*
> *will be able to quench all the fiery darts of the*
> *wicked one. And take the helmet of salvation, and*
> *the sword of the Spirit, which is the word of God.*
> —Eph. 6:13–17

I have spent hours standing at my closet doors, looking at what's inside. The clothes never seem to do what I want them to do on my body, but I go to great lengths to ensure that I am properly clothed each day.

At times, nothing feels right! I hate the way those pants look in the front. That shirt itches. This outfit makes me look huge, and that one is my worst color! In the end, I usually end up wearing the very first article of clothing that I chose.

Sadly, I do not invest nearly as much time in making sure that my soul is well covered. I am concerned that I wear just the right clothes to make me comfortable in any weather, but I leave the most important parts of me unprotected.

Father, teach me to dress from the inside out!

You shall not bow down to them nor serve them.
For I, the LORD your God, am a jealous God,
visiting the iniquity of the fathers upon the children
to the third and fourth generations of those who
hate Me.
                                        —Deut. 5:9

Throughout my treatment I have felt like I was dealing with my issues on two planes. The hurts from my past had to be faced, and my current habits had to be evaluated because I am a mother. It hurt me to realize that I was passing along to my children the same wounds that caused me grief.

My biggest fear is that my children will turn out like me. I do not want all my inadequacies and weaknesses passed along to another generation! I know that some of the ways that my parents dealt with food were unhealthy, and yet I see myself making the same mistakes!

God knows that I do not want my children to be paranoid about fat, obsessed with food, afraid of germs, or compulsive in their behavior.

I have taken steps to break the destructive patterns in my life, and I am continuing to make progress in my recovery. My children are aware that I don't like the way I deal with food; I tell them that the way I do things is not always right. I hope that, as I get healthier, they will be able to follow my new footsteps toward wholeness.

Father, protect my children from my mistakes! Let my generation be a new start for this family.

> *For He satisfies the longing soul,*
> *And fills the hungry soul with goodness.*
> —Ps. 107:9

For thirteen years I tried to fill up my emptiness myself. I always thought I was hungry, but no matter how much I ate, I couldn't make the pain stop. There was still a dull, aching void inside me.

At times I became completely obsessed with food. I figured that I just was not eating the right food. Cooking elaborate gourmet menus that took much time and expense still did not fill my hungry soul. Searching for new and different restaurants was a costly venture, too, but I still felt empty.

I began compulsively shopping. I reasoned that I had been looking in the wrong places, so maybe clothes would make me feel better. After accumulating a huge credit card debt, I realized that clothes were not the answer.

For some time, I busied myself with many different activities, thinking that I just had too much free time on my hands. I hoped that getting involved would fix me. I became active in church, got a part-time job, did catering on the side, and sold a popular line of cosmetics—in addition to being a mother and wife.

After I had exhausted all my options, I came to the realization that God was the only one who could fill my empty heart. Nothing else had worked!

Lord, help me stop trying to fill your spot in my soul.

*Inasmuch as many have undertaken to compile an
account of the things accomplished among us.*
—Luke 1:1 NAS

There came a point during treatment for my eating
disorder when I became discouraged. It was so easy to
see what still needed to be done, but I struggled to find
the positive changes I had made. My therapist asked
me to make a list of all the things I had accomplished
since entering Remuda Ranch.

I avoided the assignment for as long as I could and
then started the task at the last minute. Acknowledging my attributes and abilities was very painful for me;
I had spent my life believing that I was unable to do
anything worthwhile. With a big piece of paper and
colorful markers, I made a list of what had taken place,
and I was amazed to watch as the list grew!

Today as I looked at the calendar I realized I entered
treatment exactly one year ago. I still look at the areas
that need work; it's always easy for me to dwell on the
negative side of life. However, it is not as hard now for
me to accept my accomplishments. That's one big
change! I also see months of abstinence from disordered eating stretching out behind me, and I am
very grateful for that.

*Father, when I look at the ledger now, my account looks pretty good!
Thank you.*

> *Yea, though I walk through the valley of*
> *the shadow of death,*
> *I will fear no evil;*
> *For You are with me;*
> *Your rod and Your staff, they comfort me.*
> —Ps. 23:4

I had always feared being abandoned until one day when I was studying this familiar psalm. The whole chapter took on new meaning that day. But one phrase in particular, "Your rod and Your staff, they comfort me" stood out.

I learned that the shepherd uses his rod to guide, protect, count, and rescue his sheep. Knowing that God is my Shepherd and that he guides, protects, and rescues me is wonderful. The idea that I am important enough to be counted thrilled me even more!

God sees me as one of his sheep. I am of enough value to him that he counts me and watches to make sure that I stay close. If I stray my Good Shepherd will come and find me.

When fearful thoughts threaten to take over, I gain comfort by remembering that God is my Shepherd. Then I feel loved and secure.

Thank you, Good Shepherd, for lovingly guiding me. Please keep me safe and close to you.

For everyone who asks receives, and he who seeks finds, and to him who knocks it will be opened.
—Matt. 7:8

While I was in treatment for my eating disorder I met many women who were desperately seeking to get well. I gained strength by watching them as they plowed through their fears and faced themselves.

At times I wanted to run away from the pain! It seemed like I could not bear the emotional strain, and I wanted to give up. I know that others shared my feelings; we struggled to encourage each other in the midst of our own pain.

It hurt me so much to see my friends in agony as they pursued wholeness. But that was not nearly as sad as watching the women who were unwilling to get better. Some were so afraid of what was under the food obsession that they would not give up the external behaviors long enough to look inside.

Some women had been in countless inpatient treatment centers, yet they were still totally focused on food. They never got past the symptoms to look at the real problems.

I have been encouraged as I see many of my friends making progress in their recovery. We aren't doing perfectly, but as we honestly seek to get well the doors of healing continue to open.

Father, thank you for giving me the desire to continue seeking wholeness.

> *When I was a child, I spoke as a child, I*
> *understood as a child, I thought as a child; but*
> *when I became a man, I put away childish things.*
> —1 Cor. 13:11

A therapist once told me that my emotional growth stopped when I started hiding from life behind my eating disorder. She said I stopped maturing when I started numbing out. Unfortunately, I think she is right.

I'm twenty-nine years old, but I'm only fifteen on the inside. I have responsibilities as a wife, a mom, and a working woman, but I am sadly lacking in the emotional stability to deal with those things.

When the stress level gets too high, I can't handle it. I deal with things pretty well for a teenager, but not acceptably as an adult. My heart is too sensitive! Disappointment does me in.

Fortunately I no longer use food to bury my fears. I don't numb out when my feelings get hurt; I have to deal with the pain.

My desire is to let God change me into the woman he wants me to be. I think it's time to grow up!

Father, thank you for preserving my life long enough to give me time to grow.

But Ruth said:
"Entreat me not to leave you,
Or to turn back from following after you;
For wherever you go, I will go;
And wherever you lodge, I will lodge;
Your people shall be my people,
And your God, my God.   —Ruth 1:16

Ruth was so committed to caring for her mother-in-law that she was willing to leave her country and her people behind to follow Naomi.

For some time, this passage of Scripture has been my prayer to the Lord. I have said, "Yes, Lord, I am willing to leave everything that is comfortable and familiar to follow you." This means leaving behind my drive to have a perfect body. I have given up trying to control what I want to weigh; I have asked God what weight he designed me to be.

This is so difficult! I fear that giving up my eating-disordered ways will make me fat. I am afraid that God's plan for me includes more weight than I want. I know this does not make sense logically, but I'm convinced that my punishment for abusing my body is being fat. The irrational part of me says, "After all, that's what you deserve!"

I want my heart to be like Ruth's. I choose to follow God with no strings attached. I will trust him to do what he thinks is best for me; I know deep in my heart that God will not harm me. His love for me is complete and unconditional. That means I won't get the punishment that I "deserve."

Lord, enable me to trust you fully!

> *And do not be conformed to this world, but be*
> *transformed by the renewing of your mind, that you*
> *may prove what is that good and acceptable and*
> *perfect will of God.*
> —Rom. 12:2

I call them my "voices"; other people call them "old tapes." Whatever they're called, I'm referring to the ugly, destructive thoughts that plague me. Sometimes those voices get so loud that I can't even think straight! The ideas in my head get pretty scary.

The thoughts would completely destroy me if I allowed them. I have learned that I have to take drastic measures to stop the voices from talking in my head.

One way I have successfully stilled them is to say out loud, "Jesus, help me!" This used to alarm my family, but I explained to them that when I struggled with my thoughts, that's what I needed to do. It seems pretty silly, maybe even embarrassing, but it works for me.

Sometimes I turn inspirational music on very loudly to drown out the bad thoughts. I've found that reading encouraging letters from friends over and over again gives me good things to think about. It's still hard for me to say good things about myself, but I can accept affirmations from others. Remembering that I am loved and accepted by God transforms my thinking!

Father, fill my mind with thoughts of your love. Please protect me from horrible thoughts.

For it would have been better for us to serve the Egyptians than that we should die in the wilderness.

—Ex. 14:12

Some days recovery feels like wandering in the wilderness; I struggle to find the way. The path seems to be covered with a tangle of bushes and thorns; I'm not sure what lies ahead!

Like the author of today's verse, I sometimes want to go back. I convince myself that it really wasn't that bad back in "Egypt." Yes, I was killing myself with my eating disorder, but now I'm sure I could control things if I went back!

I hate having to face the unknown; my faith is weak. The pain of recovery feels overwhelming, and anything would be better than the way I feel right now!

Going back is never the answer. Recovery symbolizes moving forward. This path may not always be clear; there are unknown hazards up ahead, but I know what lies behind me! I have gone back to visit "Egypt," and each time it's much worse than I remembered. As hard as it seems, it's better to keep moving forward.

Lord, when I start grumbling and complaining about recovery, please remind me where I used to be!

> *I say to you, if you have faith as a mustard seed, you will say to this mountain, "Move from here to there," and it will move; and nothing will be impossible for you.*
> —Matt. 17:20

The faith of a child is a beautiful thing. Children love their parents and trust them with their lives unquestioningly. Children always believe their parents are doing what's right and best for them.

I know I am a child of God, so why don't I trust him? I want to dig down deep into my well of faith and relax in the love of my Father.

If there are things in my life that keep me from trusting God, I will work through them so I may be free to draw on his strength.

Today I will say, "Lord, here is my life; I put it back in your hands. Teach me; guide me; love me." I will take my little mustard seed of faith and let it grow into a field of flowers.

Lord, let my faith bloom in your love.

*For you were bought at a price; therefore glorify
God in your body and in your spirit, which are
God's.*
                                        —1 Cor. 6:20

I used to believe that to glorify God with my body, I
had to look like a model. I spent years dieting for the
Lord. I thought that being thin would enhance my relationship with him since I would no longer feel the need
to hide.

I went to many extremes trying to attain the perfect
body. I abused laxatives and diuretics, and I often
threw up everything I ate. I constantly told myself, "I'll
start doing more for the Lord when I look good
enough."

That day never came. Driven by my obsession, I
never felt thin enough. My shame over the way I
looked caused me to withdraw into myself and away
from God. I thought my looks made me unlovable.

I decided that since God loves me and accepts me, I
can do the same. When I abuse my body I do not bring
glory to him. Having a firm body would only bring
glory to me.

I believe that God wants me to be physically fit, but I
now know that his deepest desire is that I become spiritually healthy.

_____

Lord, help me stop abusing my body and start bringing glory to you.

Diverse weights are an abomination to the LORD,
And dishonest scales are not good.

—Prov. 20:23

Soon after I left treatment for my eating disorder I began playing the "scale game." Each morning I got on the scale with nothing on at all. It was a big gamble! With a spin of the dial, I could determine the entire outcome of my day!

The number was never good enough. If the scale said I weighed more than I had the day before, it was enough to send me crawling back to bed. On the days when I weighed less, I felt as if I should have lost even more weight.

My obsession with the scale got out of hand. One day I even stopped at two different medical offices to weigh on my way to the therapist's office! I had never been to either of these offices before, and needless to say, I have not been back since.

Finally I made a choice not to allow my scale to determine my worth any longer. With all my might, I slammed the sacred scale down on my back porch! I felt such a release. After that, my son and a few of his friends got a hammer and a screw driver and took the scales completely apart. It is powerless over me now.

These days, I weigh only at my therapist's office, every other week. I am learning, little by little, to look to God each day to determine my worth.

Lord, thanks for loving me no matter what I weigh!

Peace I leave with you, My peace I give to you; not as the world gives do I give to you. Let not your heart be troubled, neither let it be afraid.
—John 14:27

The storms of life rage around me and inside me. I feel unsettled and anxious; I am engulfed in a sea of fear. It seems like no one understands how I feel. There is no rest, no relief for me. Where is the peace I was promised?

I would like all my problems to be eliminated entirely, but God never said that life would be easy. He did promise to comfort me with his peace during the trials.

God's peace does not always come in the form I expect. The peace he gives is the same kind he gave his Son Jesus. It was an all-encompassing peace; it allowed him to endure the pain and humiliation of death on the cross. My circumstances seem overwhelming at times, but nothing I have to face is as painful as crucifixion. In the midst of the storms of life, God's peace will be my guide.

————————

Lord, I thank you for your ever-present peace.

How long, you simple ones, will you love simplicity?
—Prov. 1:22

For many years I dealt with life in black and white. Things were either yes or no, all or none. It seemed very simple to me this way, and I gained a sense of security from my rigidity. I was unable to see any middle ground, any gray area.

Since I could not be the thinnest woman in the world, I allowed myself to eat everything in sight, until I felt like the fattest woman anywhere. I had trouble eating sweets in moderation, so I completely eliminated sugar from my diet.

My extreme ways of thinking carried over into every area of my life. Since I was not perfect and could not keep all of God's laws, I reasoned that surely I could not be a Christian.

My views of others were narrow-minded as well. If a friend could not be completely devoted to me all the time, I figured that she was no friend at all. My parents did not raise me without making mistakes, so in my mind, they weren't fit to be parents.

Even in my eating disorder, I felt betrayed because there were always women who were worse off than I was. I couldn't even manage to be the best bulimic in the world!

God is teaching me that things are not always simple; I don't have to be the best or the worst at everything I do.

———————

Father, teach me to accept the gray areas.

Or do you not know that your body is the temple of the Holy Spirit who is in you, whom you have from God, and you are not your own?

—1 Cor. 6:19

Imagine this: I took twelve to fifteen laxatives each day, downed prescription diuretics every other day, consumed three times my regular dosage of thyroid medication daily, and vomited every bite of food that passed my lips. This is how I cared for the temple of the Holy Spirit!

I hated myself, and I hated my body. I despised what God had created. It was as if I said to God, "I could do a better job if I were given the chance!" Growing up in a family with secrets caused me to be fearful and full of shame. Many of those feelings came to the surface in the form of an obsession with my body.

I am gradually learning to accept how God designed me, inside and out. I am the temple for his Spirit. My legs may not be as long as I'd like, and after having three children, my stomach is no longer flat. I am still God's creation, and I am worthy to house his Holy Spirit because Christ lives in me!

Lord, when I am tempted to hate my body, remind me that I belong to you.

Yet you do not have because you do not ask.
—James 4:2

My first few weeks at the treatment center for eating disorders found me terribly homesick. It was the last place in the world I wanted to be. I was confused and seemed to be getting nowhere.

Recovery was difficult and perplexing, but I wanted to be well with all my heart. I realized that I was not asking God for his guidance. Since my way did not seem to be working, I made the choice to ask the Lord to lead me in recovery.

Each morning I would look to God for directions for my day. "What things do you want me to deal with today, Lord? What is your plan for my eating?" As I prayed, he directed my heart and gave me insight on his plan.

God never left me wandering aimlessly, not knowing what to do or how to do it. Recovery became exciting as I followed the Lord down the path to my healing!

I had always thought today's verse referred to material needs. But I realized that God is concerned with every area of my life. He has given me a lot as I have learned to ask!

Lord, remind me that when I lack something, I can turn to you for help.

*But encourage one another day after day, as long
as it is still called "Today," lest any one of you be
hardened by the deceitfulness of sin.*
                                    —Heb. 3:13 NAS

During the worst days of my eating disorder, I isolated myself from people. I did not want to be around others because I thought I was fat; I tried to hide my inadequacies. I did not believe I had anything to offer, and I did not want to bother people.

Looking back I realize that in isolation I could not give or receive encouragement. I cut myself off from all support. I found it difficult to ask for help, because I hated to risk being rejected. Instead, I separated myself from others and wallowed in my loneliness. No one knew my needs.

I robbed myself of many blessings, and I cheated others when I refused to share myself. Because I was so wrapped up in my own pain, I was not available to God either.

This road to recovery is not meant to be traveled solo! This verse talks of encouraging one another day after day, but that is not possible if I keep myself hidden.

Lord, give me the courage to step outside myself and share encouragement with others.

> *Now do not be stiff-necked, as your fathers were,*
> *but yield yourselves to the LORD.*
> —2 Chron. 30:8

As I began my recovery I was like an unbroken horse. I did not want the bit in my mouth, and I fought against the reins. I wanted to do things my way!

Some horses, even after being broken, never accept the bit and the reins. They remain obstinate and uncooperative; these horses cannot be trained to respond to a rider's commands.

I have been unresponsive to the reins of recovery at times. Doctors and therapists have given me ideas on how to become healthy, but I refuse to yield to their advice.

Part of the prescription is a balanced food plan, but because I am fearful of becoming fat, I refuse to follow the guidelines. I often wonder why I am not progressing more rapidly in my recovery!

Recovery is a process of yielding; I must be willing to comply, to submit, and to give way if I want to be healthy. I must be willing to surrender myself to a plan that is not like my own. I choose to surrender control of my recovery. I will submit to those who know what is best for me and comply with the program.

Father, soften my neck to the reins of recovery.

*Every good gift and every perfect gift is from above,
and comes down from the Father of lights, with
whom there is no variation or shadow of turning.*
—James 1:17

Since I have an eating disorder, meals are not always a pleasurable experience. I struggle to keep my emotions and my food separate, but it is so difficult! There are times when it is a battle to swallow each bite.

Intellectually I know that food is good for my body, and that without it I would die. But I hate my need for food; I want to do without it.

When I read this verse, God gave me the idea of visualizing food as little gifts, beautifully wrapped and bearing a tag saying, "From God, with love." I try to view my meals as a party, and I accept each bite as a present from God. It's hard to refuse gifts that my heavenly Father lovingly prepares and gives to me.

Now when eating is difficult, I remind myself that the gift of my life and health depends on my acceptance of God's gift of food. I'm thankful for the gifts that come to me from God, the giver of good things.

Lord, help me remember that food is a gift from you!

> *By faith Abraham obeyed when he was called to go out to the place which he would receive as an inheritance. And he went out, not knowing where he was going.*
> —Heb. 11:8

The Lord promised Abraham an inheritance. To receive it, he had to leave everything he knew. Abraham obeyed, although he did not know what the future held for him. He trusted that God would fulfill his promise.

I was called to recovery in the same way. It is the land of my inheritance, but the journey is long and hard. As I stepped out in faith, I had no idea what would take place. Like Abraham, I chose to trust God to be with me through the process.

I can imagine that it was painful for Abraham to leave his home and belongings and start out for an unknown destination. It was difficult for me to leave the comfort and security of my eating disorder, although I knew it was slowly killing me. I wondered, "What is my destination? Will I struggle only to fail again?"

Abraham took a risk, uprooting his family to move to an unknown place. By faith, he obeyed God and received his inheritance. I, too, am choosing to obey my calling and step out in faith; I will receive my inheritance of health.

Lord, strengthen my faith so I may continue to obey you and progress in my recovery.

For now we see in a mirror, dimly, but then face to face. Now I know in part, but then I shall know just as I also am known. —1 Cor. 13:12

Therapists tell me that fat is not a feeling, but I have trouble accepting that fact. I wake up many mornings just feeling fat!

If I look at myself closely in the mirror, I seem to get fatter by the minute. I try to avoid the mirror altogether, because I know I don't see myself the way others see me. I don't have an accurate view.

Even though I have lost lots of weight, I have a hard time seeing myself as anything but an enormous, fat woman. My clothes sizes have changed; I'm buying them in a new department! But I still have an image of myself tipping the scales at 238 lbs.

My fat was part of me for so many years that my brain is struggling to adjust to the new physical picture of me. It seems to be just as hard for my heart to accept the differences inside me. I long for a clear picture of this new me.

I know that I can only see a few of the changes in the mirror, but I'm working to get a new view of myself. Attempting to accept compliments from others, giving myself affirmations, and concentrating on how God views me are ways I can see myself clearly.

_____

Father, help me see myself accurately through you!

> *Now godliness with contentment is great gain. For*
> *we brought nothing into this world, and it is certain*
> *we can carry nothing out.* —1 Tim. 6:6–7

I have such trouble being content with my body! My dissatisfaction with myself drives me to continually work on looking perfect. I believe that if I look perfect, then my life will be problem-free! I spend countless hours and money trying to achieve my standard of perfection. I never attain it; I am never satisfied.

I expend so much on my outward appearance that I neglect my inner self. When I exercise two or three hours each day, there is no time left for quiet moments with the Lord. If I spend thousands of dollars to improve myself surgically, it cuts into what is available to give to the Lord's work.

My body is only a temporary vessel; it will age and die and eventually return to dust. My heart is eternal! While I am obsessed with being thin and looking perfect, I am neglecting to tend to the part of me that will last forever.

When my priorities are right and I am seeking to do what is important to God, then I experience true contentment.

Dear Jesus, help me find contentment in you.

For bodily exercise profits a little, but godliness is profitable for all things, having promise of the life that now is and of that which is to come.
—1 Tim. 4:8

I read this exhortation to train myself to be godly. I am beginning to invest time and effort into becoming healthier emotionally and spiritually.

Usually I don't have time or energy to exercise my soul; I am too busy perfecting my appearance. I boast when I am able to abstain from eating meat for a week, and I revel in my ability to exercise for an hour each day. When I restrict my intake of food all day, I gain a sense of power.

Society gives acclaim to those who are able to eat only salad and exercise for hours at a time. People say, "Look at how well-disciplined she is." I believe that I am a failure because I am lacking in that kind of discipline.

Pursuing wholeness internally will have value for me today, tomorrow, and forever. Godliness is not dependent on what I weigh or how I look. The number on the scale doesn't count in the life to come!

Lord, help me pursue what is of value to you.

> *All things are lawful for me, but all things are not helpful. All things are lawful for me, but I will not be brought under the power of any.*
>
> —1 Cor. 6:12

Part of learning to eat normally is being aware of certain foods that trigger an emotional response in me. If I know that eating a candy bar is going to make me feel guilty, I can choose to avoid candy bars. Feeling guilty and fat can lead me to return to bingeing and purging.

I have learned that guilt is a big factor in why I avoid certain foods. Since I do not look like a fashion model, I do not feel worthy of eating food that is not necessary for my survival. I worry about what people are going to think if they see me eating something just for enjoyment.

In the early stages of my recovery I stuck to my food plan rigidly. Doing that gave me a sense of security and that was what I needed at that point. These days I feel a little more free to take risks with food. But I keep in mind that even though I can eat what I want, some foods are not helpful in my long-range goals for weight and health.

Father, I'm thankful for freedom with food.

*But you are a chosen generation, a royal
priesthood, a holy nation, His own special people,
that you may proclaim the praises of Him who
called you out of darkness into His marvelous light.*
—1 Peter 2:9

Today I saw some of my writing in print. I noticed that I had ended a sentence in a preposition and some of the punctuation was not done properly. I felt awful! My chest was tight and I felt sick to my stomach. I had to make a phone call to a friend and talk through my obsessive thoughts.

The problem is that when I make a mistake I see myself as a failure. I am still so insecure that having my shortcomings made public is humiliating to me. My friend said, "Get a grip! So you forgot some of the rules of English—does it really matter in the long run?" I need people to help me put things in perspective when my thinking gets out of control.

I still tend to base my value on my performance. I have to remind myself that God loves me no matter how I spell. I am chosen by him; he considers me special even if I end a sentence in a preposition.

Lord, help me get a grip on your love for me!

> *Come now, you who say, "Today or tomorrow we*
> *will go to such and such a city, spend a year there,*
> *buy and sell, and make a profit"; whereas you do*
> *not know what will happen tomorrow.*
> —James 4:13–14

I often act like I have control over everything in my life. It is hard to accept that I can't even control what will happen in the next few minutes, let alone how my life will turn out.

What I get for all my planning and worrying is a false sense of security and disappointment when things don't go as planned. I once heard someone say, "I know I can't control the ocean tides, but watch me try!"

On a tubing trip this summer, my friend and I decided it would be a good time to stop for lunch. We were about half way down the river, and the water was flowing very rapidly. But we were determined to have lunch right then, so we jumped off the tubes and attempted to stand up against the heavy current.

Our efforts lasted several minutes as we were dragged over huge boulders in the river! We ended up scraped up, discouraged, and even more hungry than we were in the beginning!

I am learning to take control of things that I can control and let go of the delusion that I have power over anything else. _____

Father, thank you for not laughing out loud at my attempts to gain control of my life!

MOVING TOWARD JOY

Lord, let your words
Weave a unique design
Of color
Into the garment of my life.

May your hands lead me
To a sincere way of living,
In a world that
Is not always pure.

Help me to accept
The power of your Spirit,
As I move through
The joys and pains
Of each new day.

Renew my faithfulness to you
And strengthen me,
To love those
Who need you the most.

July 2 – LISTEN UP!

Listen to counsel and receive instruction,
That you may be wise in your latter days.
—Prov. 19:20

I find that often when I talk I don't want to listen to what anybody has to say about my thoughts. I share myself, but I am resistant to feedback. I am aware of how distorted my thinking can be, but it is hard to hear the truth.

When I am talking harshly about myself, many of my friends will correct me. I have asked to be reminded when my words are self-deprecating, but it is difficult to believe people when they say good things about me.

Changing my eating-disordered thought patterns is the biggest struggle I face in my recovery. I have already decided what I will believe, and it is hard to accept new thinking.

I am making a conscious effort to listen to the advice of those trusted few who are part of my team. When my therapist points out areas that are still lacking, I fight the feelings of failure and rejection. As I ask my nutritionist for advice on my food plan, I accept her advice on my eating.

None of this is easy, but my own plan was not working well. Reminding myself of this makes it a little easier to listen to counsel.

Father, I ask that you make my heart willing to receive the wisdom others have to offer.

Your ears shall hear a word behind you, saying,
"This is the way, walk in it,"
Whenever you turn to the right hand
Or whenever you turn to the left. —Isa. 30:21

God, help me! Show me how to stop this crazy dieting!" I can't even recall how many times I said this. Over the years of lying about food, I found myself becoming less and less in tune with God.

My prayers and quiet times grew dead and meaningless. The longer I knowingly disobeyed God, the more spiritually deaf I became. As I continued to ignore his promptings, it became easier to make poor choices without feeling any remorse.

Now that I'm in recovery I am trying to stay honest, especially with my food plan. I find myself hearing God's directions more clearly; he leads me away from temptation and toward healthy choices.

As I'm learning to walk closely with God, I've found that he is willing to direct me. My part is to be willing to listen and obey his voice. I'm thankful that no matter which way I turn, God is right along with me.

God, thank you for your guidance.

The Spirit of the LORD GOD is upon Me,
Because the LORD has anointed Me
To preach good tidings to the poor;
He has sent Me to heal the brokenhearted,
To proclaim liberty to the captives,
And the opening of the prison to those
*   who are bound.*
                                        —Isa. 61:1

For years I was a prisoner in bondage to eating disorders. I could not get free of the distorted thinking that plagued me. I was haunted by feelings of inadequacy and unworthiness.

Much of my life was used up trying to run from the pain. I busied myself trying to please others in order to feel better about myself. I based my entire worth on the opinions of those around me; I allowed them to determine my value.

The scariest prison of all was the eating disorder; it totally controlled my life. For a time I refused to eat at all, but that did not last long. When I finally allowed myself to eat, I could not do so in a normal manner. I found myself consuming huge quantities of food.

Christ came to set me free from all my prisons. He is healing my broken heart of the memories of sexual abuse. He has freed me from my obsession with food so that I can learn how to deal with my pain. He can bring freedom to your life, too!

Father, I long to be free! Please continue to break down the walls of my prisons.

I beseech you therefore, brethren, by the mercies of God, that you present your bodies a living sacrifice, holy, acceptable to God, which is your reasonable service.
—Rom. 12:1

Good morning, Lord!

I want you to take all of me and use me in this new day! I offer myself to you.

I give you my mind. Please take control of my thoughts and make them pleasing to you. Thank you for my intellect. Help me to use it to accomplish what you have planned for my day.

Father, take control of my mouth. Please make the words that come out of it kind and loving. Give me the ability to say honest words. Thank you for the pleasure of eating good food.

Here are my arms and my hands. Thank you for making them whole and usable. It feels so good to hold others and to be held. I ask that the work I accomplish this day will bring glory to you.

I offer you my insides, Lord. Please protect my heart from the pain around me today.

Thank you for my strong legs and feet. Lord, direct my steps today so that I will be where you want me to be. Thank you for the ability to run and play.

Lord, I give myself to you. Please make me willing to be part of your plan.

> *He is a double-minded man, unstuble in all*
> *his ways.*
> —James 1:8

Today I am afraid that I am going to meet a deadline! If I accomplish this task, I fear the expectations that will follow. I will no longer be able to believe the lies that I have told myself for years. I might just have to accept the fact that I am a capable and worthwhile human being!

Two sides of me are constantly warring against each other. Part of me is so afraid of failure that I resist any risks that might result in rejection. The other side of me is so afraid of success that I struggle not to sabotage my accomplishments.

The fear of failure is terrifying to me, but I realize now that success is equally hard to face. There is not much pressure living life as a failure; it is pretty easy to measure up to no standard at all.

Success means that I will have to change my belief system about who I am. The old script I have written in stone will have to be smashed.

Stability is coming slowly in my recovery, as I strive to clear my mind of the old picture of me.

Father, teach me to be single-minded and stable.

Do you not know that those who run in a race all run, but one receives the prize? Run in such a way that you may obtain it.
—1 Cor. 9:24

This race I'm in is no game! The battle is against an eating disorder, and the prize is life. I constantly have to ask myself, "Am I doing everything I can to win?"

There are many times when it seems easier to give in to old habits. I have to remind myself that those old habits almost cost me my life. It is costly to allow myself to take my recovery lightly.

At times I do not take time out to eat; I get busy and don't want to bother with food. It doesn't seem like a major offense, but when I am overly hungry at the next meal, it could mean the start of a binge. In order to run the race to win, I follow the food plan that keeps my body functioning.

Going to support groups is not always thrilling, but when I miss meetings, I get discouraged and am more susceptible to getting off track. Taking time out for my recovery is part of running this race to win.

If I push myself to do everything just right I get tired and irritable. A lack of sleep and time for recreation makes it hard to win the race. No matter what, I will continue to run this race for the prize of life.

Father, I want to win the race!

> *"Peace I leave with you, My peace I give to you; not as the world gives do I give to you. Let not your heart be troubled, neither let it be afraid."*
>
> —John 14:27

I was raised on a farm in Silverton, Oregon, and when we sold it I felt lost. Though my home life was like a silent war, I found serenity in the coolness of the mountains. I loved the outdoors, choosing walks in the forest over nights in the city.

Peace was available to me in God's creation. When the pain got so great that I needed to cry, I would find a quiet spot outside, bury my head in my lap, and weep. My tears were not welcome in our home.

When I moved to the city, I did not know how to find peace; I felt stripped of the little peace I had. Bulimia became the outlet for my pain, and soon it began to destroy my dreams.

Now I am recovering from my addiction to food. I find my peace in God, others, and little things that bring me joy. Some days my heart lets me know that there are more tears to be shed. Grieving old losses is vital for my growth and healing.

Lord, fill me with your peace; nourish my soul with your presence. Please teach me to open up to others.

*But reject profane and old wives' fables, and
exercise yourself toward godliness.*

—1 Tim. 4:7

Where did I get the idea that I cannot eat meat? Why can't I drink milk with fish? Who says I can't mix fruits and proteins at the same meal? Can I really expect never to consume sugar again? What makes me think I will get fat if I eat three well-balanced meals each day?

My ideas about eating have come from a variety of sources. I learned recently that one of my uncles choked on a fish bone while he was drinking milk, so my family has avoided the combination of fish and milk at the same meal. Talk about a wives' tale!

Some of my irrational beliefs regarding food are not so easy to trace, but I am trying to let go of my obsessive thoughts on food. I want to eat properly so my body functions well, and I have found that I can do that without feeling deprived!

In the last year I have been following a food plan prescribed by my nutritionist. It is well-balanced and allows me to eat the foods I like. I am able to enjoy food more now, and am learning that food is not something to be feared!

Lord, help me to let go of the lies about food.

> *And Jesus answered and said to her, "Martha,*
> *Martha, you are worried and troubled about*
> *many things."*
> —Luke 10:41

I hate to admit it, but I'm a lot like Martha, especially when I'm expecting company. No matter how much time and effort I spend on cleaning, it's never enough.

My family dreads having company because they know it means I'll be in a cleaning frenzy for days before the guests arrive. I lose all objectivity; everything else is forgotten except the urgent need to put the house in perfect order.

I have learned so much from my friend Karen. Her house is open to anybody at all hours of the day or night. She works and is busy with her family and church activities, so her house is rarely in perfect shape. She just doesn't sweat the small stuff!

Karen's attitude is one I envy. Relationships are more important to her than cleaning, and she makes time for friends and family. Amazingly, people seem to enjoy themselves; they feel relaxed and welcome in her home.

I am working to become more like Karen and less like Martha. I remind myself that my worth is not dependent on the way my house looks.

Lord, teach me to worry less about the little stuff.

Therefore they shall eat the fruit of their own way,
And be filled to the full with their own fancies.
—Prov. 1:31

My eating disorder "career" started with anorexia, but although I liked being thin, I hated feeling hungry. I soon learned that I could eat what I wanted and not gain weight by throwing up. It seemed like a great way to keep my weight under control.

When I was confronted with my purging I stopped doing it. I was not able to stop eating compulsively, though. Now I know there was secret pain hidden underneath my obsession with food.

For years I ate everything in sight, and my weight got completely out of control. It did not seem to matter at the time. I hated myself when I was thin, and I hated myself when I was fat.

There came a point in time when I had my fill of food. I was also aware that I could not go on living the way I was, because my life was in danger. I wondered back then why God didn't intervene. It was as if I expected him to reach down and take the food out of my mouth. I have since learned that I was not willing to receive his help until I was sure I could not fix myself.

Lord, I am so thankful that you saved me until I had my fill and was willing to ask for help.

> *And do not lead us into temptation, but deliver us
> from the evil one.*
> —Matt. 6:13

The first few months out of treatment were extremely painful. It took constant effort not to slip back into the old unhealthy habits. I struggled daily to eat just what I was supposed to, no more and no less.

One morning was especially difficult; I remember crying for hours because I was not sure I could keep up the effort. At that time, in my weakened state, I heard the doorbell ring.

A smiling Girl Scout greeted me as I opened the door. It was time for their annual cookie sale! After she had made her sales pitch, she said apologetically, "All I have left are three boxes of the peanut butter kind." I couldn't believe my ears—they are my all-time favorite cookies!

I left her at the door while I made a dash for cash inside. As I was frantically gathering up change I got a look at myself in the mirror, and I did not like what I saw. I asked myself, "So how are those cookies going to help me feel any better?"

Reluctantly I sent the Girl Scout on her way, with all three boxes of peanut butter cookies still in tow. I was amazed at what had happened. I felt as though the devil himself had just tempted me, with the one thing that was almost irresistible. But I had been given the strength to resist!

———————————

Thank you, Father, for the power to say no.

And be sure your sin will find you out.
—Num. 32:23

One day my family and I were playing a board game on the floor. My son excused himself to use the bathroom but soon rushed back into the living room. He said excitedly, "Mom, you've got to come see what's in the toilet!" And then he proceeded to describe it in vivid detail.

I became agitated and then angry as he continued because I knew very well what was in the toilet; I had purged my lunch just before joining the family. He had uncovered my secret. I was ashamed and humiliated as I tried to come up with an alibi.

As painful as it was, God used my son's discovery to propel me into recovery. I had kept the secret for so long that it was almost a relief when it was disclosed! I realized that my disease had become unmanageable; my eating disorder was controlling my life.

It has been over one year since that incident. My life is new and different since receiving treatment at Remuda Ranch. I am not the same woman I was when my son made his discovery.

Although my family was not aware of the disease that was slowly killing me, God knew all along. He saw my pain when I thought I only had an "eating problem." My secrets and shame were not news to him, but he loved me anyway!

Lord, I'm glad I got "found out" so I could get well.

> *And for this purpose also I labor, striving according to His power, which mightily works within me.*
> —Col. 1:29 NAS

Many times I have tried to change a part of my personality that I disliked. I worked and struggled, with no results! I thought the answer was turning things over to God and letting him take care of the problem. I prayed, "Lord, change me," but I was still no different.

When I read this verse in the Bible, it was as if God turned on the light bulb in my head! I realized that God was not going to change me instantly, but I did not have to make the changes on my own either.

This verse also makes clear that the changes come after much hard work. The good news is that God is willing to use his marvelous power working through me to bring about change!

This same principle applies to my eating disorder. I struggle so that I may recover. I praise God that he is willing to use his infinite strength to heal me.

Lord, help me remember that we are in this thing together!

And do not seek what you should eat or what you should drink, nor have an anxious mind.
—Luke 12:29

For the thirteen years that my eating disorder controlled my life, food was my central focus. I spent many hours every day thinking about food, planning my next meal, preparing food, and then eating it. At one point, I invested hours each day watching cooking shows on television.

Before I entered treatment I made dozens of meals and froze them for my family. My husband assumed that my motive was to care for my family's needs while I was away. Truthfully, it was just part of my obsession with food. I was clinging to food for security.

I couldn't seem to get enough groceries in the house. The cupboards were already bulging, but I continued to bring more food home. It was such a relief to enter treatment and have nothing to do with food for a while! It was prepared and set in front of me; my job was simply to eat it. That break from responsibility with food freed me to look at what was causing me to be obsessed with food.

Food is slowly losing its grip on me. As I continue to work on the real problems in my life, food becomes less and less of an issue.

Lord, thank you for releasing me from the obsession with food. Remind me that food is fuel, and no more.

The end of a thing is better than its beginning.
—Eccl. 7:8

When I first left the treatment center for eating disorders, I did not think I could make it through a whole day in the real world. People kept encouraging me to live one day at a time, but the days were too long! I had to concentrate on minutes and hours.

The trauma of returning to the mainstream of life was extremely painful; it took more than I knew was in me. I learned to rely on God and to turn to others when I was tempted to quit.

As I look back over the last year of my life, I am amazed and grateful to see what has taken place. Progress is evident in many areas of my life. Some issues are still not resolved, but things are looking much more hopeful!

In the early stages of my recovery, I was still obsessed with food. It was a struggle to follow my food plan; I was tempted to eat more or less than I needed to be healthy. Now food is not so much of an issue. When I start obsessing about food or weight, I know there is something else troubling me.

Take hope! I know how painful it is to give up old, familiar behaviors because I've been there. I promise it gets easier as time passes.

Father, I am grateful for the reminder of how hard it was in the beginning; it makes me thankful for today.

Therefore a man shall leave his father and mother and be joined to his wife, and they shall become one flesh.

—Gen. 2:24

Even though I had been married over nine years, my parents were still very involved in my life. I talked to my mom on the phone almost daily, and my dad was always there to bail us out if my husband and I needed help financially. And my parents' wishes were still mine to fulfill—at least that's what I thought.

During treatment I became aware of how dependent I was on my parents' approval. I would do anything to make them happy, even if it caused friction in my marriage. When I realized the extent of our attachment I felt a lot of anger. It made me mad to see that I treated them like gods.

At one point in my recovery I asked my parents not to contact me at all. I needed to make a separation in my identity and theirs. It was painful for them, and it hurt me too. A friend told me I was going through a "parent-ectomy"; it felt like surgery without anesthesia.

The purpose of the separation was not to cause them to change. I have accepted that the way they are is the way they will always be. I needed time to work on me! It was important for me to learn not to react to their requests.

Today we are in contact again, and we are working on developing a new, healthier relationship.

Father, I ask for wisdom in relating to my parents.

Why did I come forth from the womb to see
*   labor and sorrow,*
That my days should be consumed with shame?
                                    —Jer. 20:18

I wonder what my purpose here on earth is. As I look back over my life I see that I have gone through many stages. Some of what I see is favorable, other parts I am not so proud of.

I have spent much of my life trying to be what others expected of me. I tried to please my parents, my friends, my husband, and my children. It took me thirty-three years to realize that I could really be who I wanted to be, just exactly what God intended. I don't need the approval of others to be me!

I have chosen to approach life with a positive attitude. I know now that much can be accomplished if I choose to do it with a cheerful heart. Life is not easy; I know I must face struggles and pain. It is easier now that I am being myself and not pretending.

It is exciting to learn that I can make choices, instead of allowing others to dictate what paths I take. God has given me talents and abilities that are worthwhile and valuable.

———————

My Lord, please remind me that you are near. Guide me in the right direction. You are my strength, my hope, and my reason for living.

But let your "Yes" be "Yes," and your "No," "No,"
lest you fall into judgment.   —James 5:12

I do not always give a straight answer; often I say what I think others want to hear. My word has not always been good either. I was so anxious to please everyone, I agreed to do things that were impossible.

Another way for me to avoid responsibility is by not answering at all! I fear voicing an opinion since you might not agree with me. Rather than risk rejection I avoid expressing my needs.

In parenting, it is easier to say "Maybe later, not right now," than to deal with the disappointment of my children when I tell them no. But they have learned that I do not always mean what I say!

Part of becoming whole is taking risks. As scary as it may be, I am learning to say what I mean. This is hard; it means resisting the urge to speak impulsively. If I am going to be vulnerable, I want to make sure that what comes out of my mouth is really what I believe.

I want to be taken at my word. This means I must face the fear of rejection and speak my mind.

Lord, may I be slow to speak, and mean what I say.

> *See, O LORD, that I am in distress;*
> *My soul is troubled;*
> *My heart is overturned within me,*
> *For I have been very rebellious.*
> *Outside the sword bereaves,*
> *At home it is like death.*
>
> —Lam. 1:20

Dear God,

I am at my lowest. Everyone is against me; everything I try fails. The kids are really getting on my nerves; they are noisy and messy, and they ignore my requests. My husband is gone. I have no idea when he will be home.

I don't even feel like getting dressed or taking time to look nice. I turn to food; maybe it will make me feel better. No one else is here to help!

Wait! I am telling myself lies again. You are with me, Lord; you are always there. It is so easy to overlook the one who can really help.

God, I thank you for this chance to change. Use this difficult time to mold me into what you want. Thank you for saving me! Thank you for planning things so that I do have a part in life. I do have choices.

I see you making me strong and giving me control over the things that usually control me. Continue to give me strength as I go through these changes. I want to be a woman, a wife, and a mother who is becoming whole.

In those days men will seek death and will not find it; they will desire to die, and death will flee from them.
                                                    —Rev. 9:6

As many times as I have wished to die, I was never able to follow through with it. I had considered suicide several times, but my life was spared.

It was not until I was actually close to death that I realized how precious life is to me. I had a bad reaction to a combination of drugs and was rushed to the emergency room in the middle of the night. The professionals there pumped my stomach and then filled it with charcoal to absorb the drugs that were left.

I remember the stern voice of the nurse reminding me to breathe, and I can vaguely recall hearing the doctors discussing their concern that my blood pressure would not stabilize. Even in my dazed state I knew that my life was in danger, and I was terrified.

Something inside me took over; I did not want to die! It took everything in me to continue breathing, and I made the effort to stay alive.

I view things differently since that close call; my life is valuable to me. There are still days when I feel like giving up. When I get overwhelmed and want to die, I share honestly with others who can give encouragement. I have come too far to give up now!

Father, thank you for the gift of my life.

Trust in the LORD with all your heart,
And lean not on your own
understanding;
In all your ways acknowledge Him,
And He shall direct your paths.
—Prov. 3:5–6

I often forget to ask for help. I plow ahead, doing things on my own and feeling like I can't stand the strain. It is easy to turn to food for comfort when life seems overwhelming.

I must make many decisions that have an impact on others. Sometimes I take on areas that are not rightly mine, but other times the responsibility is mine to handle. It helps to remember that I do not have to handle it alone.

I am learning to distinguish between responsibilities I must deal with and those I can delegate to others. I have become aware of how hard I try to do what's "right." It is impossible always to make the best choice, but I have seen God use even the worst situations to bring about growth in my life.

I tend to forget that God is with me. I will rely on God's strength and his wisdom, and I will trust him with the lives of those I love as well.

Lord, guide me and give me wisdom. Help me to use the mind you gave me. I ask that you allow me to support my friends and family so that they, too, become all that you want.

*"For My thoughts are not your thoughts,
Nor are your ways My ways," says the LORD.*
—Isa. 55:8

Some of my thoughts are not based on logical beliefs. I have told myself lies for so long that I now believe them. It is hard to change thought processes, but it has to be done if I want to be healthy!

My thinking often makes no sense. "I feel lonely, so I'll get a milkshake." "My friend hurt my feelings; I'll show her. I won't eat all day!" "I'm not prepared for this test, maybe a candy bar will make me feel better." "I feel guilty for eating so much—I'd better get rid of it." "Well, I already blew my food plan; I guess I'll finish this cake."

My thoughts are not God's thoughts. He furnishes me with a new start every day, even every minute. When I make poor choices, God is there to offer me a clean slate.

None of the things I did in the past made me feel better, at least not for long. There is always a price to pay for instant gratification.

Lord, help me to learn to think like you do.

> *Most men will proclaim each his own goodness,*
> *But who can find a faithful man?*
>
> —Prov. 20:6

Since I was sexually abused as a child, my fear of people is great. Consequently, I find it difficult to trust others. During treatment for my eating disorder, I worked hard to trust the professionals in the center. In my mind they had a hidden agenda; I felt like people were bent on hurting me.

Part of my recovery has been to risk trusting others with little parts of me. I try to stay open and honest, but being vulnerable is terrifying! In truth, people are only human; they will sometimes hurt me, even if it is unintentional. My tendency is to shut down; I want to retreat into myself and push others far away. Each time I get hurt, vulnerability is more of a risk.

I have learned, though, that I cannot walk alone on this path to wholeness. I need people, as much as I hate to admit it. I am willing to push through the fear of being hurt and trust people, a little bit at a time.

God is not limited by factors like time, energy, and the ability to love. He is always there for me, even when people fail to meet my needs.

Father, give me the courage to keep being open.

I acknowledged my sin to You,
And my iniquity I have not hidden.
I said, "I will confess my transgressions to the LORD,"
And You forgave the iniquity of my sin. —Ps. 32:5

Forgiving myself for my past is one of the most difficult things I have had to face in my recovery. Although I knew God had forgiven me, I couldn't accept it and feel forgiven. I still carried shame and guilt because my actions had dishonored God.

During recovery I learned that dwelling on my past does not bring honor to God. Jesus Christ died for my sins; he knew what sins I would commit, but he loved me anyway. I make Christ's death on the cross seem futile if I do not accept his forgiveness.

It helps if I picture all my shame, guilt, and sins nailed to the cross. Jesus has washed me clean! This forgiveness is available to anyone who repents of their sins and turns to God. Now my heart is so full of my relationship with Christ that there is no room left for shame!

Lord, thank you for making me clean. Help me feel as white as snow.

> *But I say to you, love your enemies, bless those who*
> *curse you, do good to those who hate you, and*
> *pray for those who spitefully use you and*
> *persecute you.*
> —Matt. 5:44

When I feel hurt, I want to take my pain out on some-one. Oddly enough, I used to punish myself when I was angry with others.

Eating everything in sight and then throwing up until my stomach ached did not hurt anyone but me! Skipping meals won't make anyone aware that you are angry at them. Going to bed for the day is not a healthy way to express feelings.

There is no way to change an eating disorder unless you look at what's "eating" you. What hurts inside that makes you want to starve yourself? What has made you feel so dirty that taking thirty laxatives is the only way to feel clean? Who are you so angry at that eating an entire cake is all you can do to push the feelings down?

I used to eat myself into oblivion, but it wasn't a great place to be once I got there. The pain was still inside and the food no longer numbed it. I do not yet want to love those who have hurt me, but I am ready to stop hurting myself for their mistakes.

God, help me find out why I am eating. Please take the desire for revenge from me; keep me safe from myself.

Hey, Lord,
Yeah, it's me again. I am feeling lonely, and my heart is still hurting. I didn't think it would take so long to be healed.

I'm so grateful for the wholeness I have experienced in the area of my eating disorder. The pain did not go away when I stopped abusing food, but it's much easier to deal with life without my head stuck in the toilet.

Lord, I really want to be whole in other areas of my life, too. My marriage is a wreck, and I don't have a whole lot of hope about the outcome of that mess. Give me hope, please! Strengthen my faith in you.

Please protect my kids during this scary time. I don't want them to end up with problems like mine. Please take care of their little hearts and keep them safe, God!

My relationship with my parents is still strained, too. I have to let go of them and trust you to work. I am not real great at trusting, as you know.

Help me get used to the changes in my body, Lord, and tell me what I need to do about my weight. Everybody has advice, but I want to hear what you think. Talk louder please!

> *Look on my right hand and see,*
> *For there is no one who acknowledges me;*
> *Refuge has failed me;*
> *No one cares for my soul.*
> *I cried out to You, O LORD:*
> *I said, "You are my refuge,*
> *My portion in the land of the living."*
> —Ps. 142:4–5

Lately I've been longing to be cared for. Many of my needs went unmet as a child, and I'm trying to make up for what I lacked.

In treatment I learned that I am responsible for making my needs known; I can't expect those I love to read my mind. It is difficult to express my needs, though, because it means admitting that I am not self-sufficient. That's probably no big surprise to others, but I have tried to convince myself that I can live comfortably without anyone else.

I find myself demanding more than people are willing or able to give me. I long to be cared for and made to feel special. I realize, though, that it is never enough. No matter how much people tell me that I am worthwhile, I still feel empty.

When I was a child I felt alone and abandoned. In prayer I have invited Jesus to be with me in those times. I can visualize him holding me in his arms.

God is my refuge today; he is there when I need him. He cares for me now, just as he always has.

Lord Jesus, help me to believe that I am well cared for by you.

*For God so loved the world that He gave His only
begotten Son, that whoever believes in Him should
not perish but have everlasting life.*

—John 3:16

I struggle with feelings of unworthiness. The fact that I
do not have a college degree is a particularly sensitive
issue.

The world tells me, "In order to be a success, to be of
value, you must have initials behind your name." Most
of my friends have had a formal education, and I often
feel inadequate around them because I do not have a
degree.

I constantly work to keep my feelings of worth in-
tact. Today God gave me the idea that I do have many
initials after my name. I did not earn them at an institu-
tion of higher learning; these honorary degrees were
bestowed on me when I asked Jesus Christ to lead my
life.

I can add to my name H.G., J.H.C., since Romans
8:17 tells me that I am an heir of God, and a joint heir
with Christ! I read in Philippians 2:15 that I now have a
B.H. That's right, I'm blameless and harmless. In Psalm
139:14, my F.W. degree is installed; it says that I am
fearfully and wonderfully made.

For now, these initials remind me that I am of value.
I would still like to get a college degree, but I don't
need one to prove my worth.

Lord, remind me that you love me as I am.

And out of the ground the LORD God made every tree grow that is pleasant to the sight and good for food. The tree of life was also in the midst of the garden, and the tree of the knowledge of good and evil.
—Gen. 2:9

Recovery from eating disorders has equipped me with much information. I attended twelve-step support groups for many months, and there I learned a lot about why people abuse food. In treatment I underwent extensive education that helped me to break free from anorexia, bulimia, and compulsive overeating.

All this new information has helped me understand myself better; I know why I chose to have an eating disorder. The knowledge I gained also helped me see the problems in my family of origin so that I can avoid recreating the same wounds in my children.

One drawback to all this learning is the insight it has given me into other people's problems. I call it a drawback because it makes me uncomfortable to see things so clearly! I feel like Superman with his X-ray vision! I try to keep in mind that God is the only one who knows the motives of the heart.

Lord, please give me wisdom and discernment.

All your children shall be taught by the LORD,
And great shall be the peace of your
children.
—Isa. 54:13

One of my greatest fears is that my children will turn out like me! I dread the thought of passing on my dysfunction to another generation. My little ones have been through a lot as I struggled with an eating disorder and depression. They have seen more pain than I would have liked for them to see.

I want to give my children the gift of a whole mother. Since I entered treatment for my eating disorder one year ago, I have been walking the path of recovery. I cannot change the ugliness of the past, but I can do my part to insure that things will be different now.

I am grateful that God my Father has been with my kids throughout this process. I trust him to care for my little ones and to protect their hearts. I also look to him for guidance so I can teach them a better way of life.

I do not want my children to grow up obsessed with food and their bodies and focused on their performance. I am changing, and I hope that the changes in me will rub off on my kids.

Father, I give you my children. Please teach me how to teach them. I ask that you protect them from my mistakes, and help me learn to forgive myself for not being a perfect parent.

JUST THIS DAY

Just this day,
Dear Lord, I pray—
Comfort
For an aching heart,
Strength
For a family's new start.
A touch,
Loving and kind,
A little bit of joy
In each day we find.
And you, Lord, by our side,
So from our pain
We no longer hide.

> *The fear of man brings a snare,*
> *But whoever trusts in the Lord*
> *shall be safe.*
>
> —Prov. 29:25

My eating disorder seems to be fueled by a fear of people. That includes an overwhelming fear of making mistakes or being noticed by others. This obsession drives me further and further into isolation. I long to be invisible and to fade into nothingness.

My entire life is ordered around avoiding people. When the fear takes over I rarely leave my house, living much like a prisoner!

Intellectually I understand that my irrational fears stem from my lack of ability to trust God. My unwillingness to surrender to him is evidence of my weak faith. Since I do not trust God to keep me safe, I believe that I must protect myself by hiding away.

Moving out of this fear takes courage. I have been able to step out in faith by surrounding myself with supportive people. I have done this gradually by taking one little step at a time.

―――――――――

Lord, please bring people into my life who can help me tear down these prison walls.

As for the saints who are on the earth,
"They are the excellent ones, in whom
is all my delight." —Ps. 16:3

For years I have told myself the same things over and over again until I think they must be true. I have convinced myself that I am not of value because external things are not up to par.

My clothes don't come from the right stores, my body is not the right shape, and I don't weigh the perfect amount. My house is not in the right neighborhood, my friends drive better cars, and my children do not always behave perfectly in public.

I have based my worth entirely on things that are out of my control! There will always be someone with a better figure, a more expensive home, or a newer car, and there's not one thing I can do to change that.

A large part of my recovery involves changing my distorted thinking. I am learning to challenge things that I used to accept as truth. How can I believe that I am of value?

Here God tells me that I am an excellent one and that he delights in me. That truth packs punch! God sees me as worthwhile no matter what shape I'm in. He is not impressed by the car I drive or what labels are in my clothes. I am perfectly acceptable to him!

Lord, help me see the errors in my thinking; teach me to value the things that are valuable to you.

> *Not that I speak in regard to need, for I have*
> *learned in whatever state I am, to be content.*
> —Phil. 4:11

It's never enough! I always want more. I have enjoyed nine months of abstinence from disordered eating, and still I'm not content. Some areas of my life still need major change, so I do not allow myself to appreciate the things in my life that are good.

I want it all; I want to be free of the eating disorder that ruled my life for thirteen years, and I want to be totally happy. In my mind, happiness is the freedom from pain, so what are the chances of feeling happy? Slim to none—life is full of pain.

In my attempt to be perfect, I have set things up so that I will never be content. I choose not to give myself credit for little accomplishments, because I fear that I will stop moving forward if I am satisfied with where I am.

Why is it easier to dwell on the negative, rather than bask in the positive? I want to learn to be content. Today I will concentrate on being grateful for the progress I have made instead of beating myself up about the areas of my life that still need work.

Father, teach me to be content but not complacent.

For I know the thoughts that I think toward you, says the LORD, thoughts of peace and not of evil, to give you a future and a hope.　　　—Jer. 29:11

As a young college student, my future seems uncertain! It is easy to get caught up in worrying about what direction my life is taking. There are so many different options that it is hard to know which one to pursue!

When I get overwhelmed by the future I sometimes try to gain some control by restricting my food intake. I feel a sense of power when I am able to control what I eat. It is a false sense of power, and I know that abusing my body will not make the future seem any brighter.

I am learning to take time out to sift through my thoughts and feelings before resorting to starving myself. Recognizing what the problems are minimizes my need for control.

I find hope in the fact that God knows what the future holds! He knows that I am truly seeking to follow him into the future. My relationship with his Son Jesus is the source of strength and hope for me.

I try to remember that God is with me as I make decisions regarding my future. I can turn to him for strength.

Lord, show me the plans you have for my future.

August 6 – BEST FRIENDS

A friend loves at all times.
—Prov. 17:17

My friend is hurting! The problems she is dealing with are going to be around for a long time. The hurts that have been inflicted on her will last a lifetime.

Since I'm her friend, I want to help. I want to make her smile and take her pain away. I wish that I could endure the pain for her; it hurts me so much to watch helplessly from the sidelines.

There are little things I can do, like sending a card to let her know that she is in my thoughts and prayers. I can say, "I'm sorry you're hurting; let me know if I can help." I can love her and accept her through this time of pain.

This brings to mind another friend I have. Jesus loves me! It hurts him to see me hurting. As my friend, he does things so I know that he is there for me in my time of pain. He uses my friends to comfort me and give me hope when I have lost mine. He gives me a beautiful sunset, and I am reminded that I have the best friend of all.

Jesus, please love my friend through me!

The Lord is near to those who have a broken heart,
And saves such as have a contrite spirit.

—Ps. 34:18

Therapy is hard, painful work! I have learned things about my past that I wish I did not know. It seems like I was better off without all these awful memories!

While I was in treatment for anorexia I dealt with several devastating events from my past. My heart broke as I experienced emotions that I had never allowed myself to feel. Many times I wondered if I would survive the pain.

God used this verse to comfort me in the midst of my fear and pain. Looking at myself in a realistic way was the hardest work I had ever done, but the Lord was with me through it all, holding me in his arms.

Facing the pain of my past was a crushing blow. I did not want to accept the things I learned, but I am thankful that God brought me through that difficult time.

God will be close to you, no matter what is breaking your heart! If your spirit has been crushed, call out to him and ask for his help.

Lord, please heal my broken heart.

> *A bruised reed he will not break,*
> *and a smoldering wick he will not snuff out.*
> —Isa. 42:3 NIV

At times the circumstances in my life seem insurmountable. I have reached the point where I wanted to give up entirely. Still, deep down inside my heart there is a glimmer of hope.

That little flicker is barely distinguishable, but it gives me the strength to call out to God for help. He has promised to be there in my time of trouble.

God has been there time and time again when I needed him. He has made my smoldering wick of hope grow into a beautiful, warm flame.

My circumstances may not change, but I can cling to the comforting knowledge that God will sustain me. He will protect my tender heart and help me to grow stronger day by day.

God, please don't let me be overwhelmed! Keep my tiny flame of hope alive. Thank you for protecting my tender heart,

*Be anxious for nothing, but in everything by prayer
and supplication, with thanksgiving, let your
requests be made known to God; and the peace
of God, which surpasses all understanding, will
guard your hearts and minds through Christ Jesus.*
—Phil. 4:6–7

My mind is spinning and my heart is aching. Every-thing seems overwhelming right now and I'm all worked up. My mind plays tricks on me; I've conjured up a big disaster from the simplest situation. I need peace!

When I am in this mode, I don't take time out for God. I don't even have time for God; I'm much too busy obsessing about impending catastrophes to ask him for help. My thinking gets so distorted that it is hard to think rationally. Even when I get the facts, I have trou-ble believing them.

What a waste of time and energy! All I manage to do is set myself up for a major fall. My obsessing controls me, and I want to control life. I get more and more anxious as I see that situations are beyond my control.

This verse says to be anxious for nothing; I am to go to God with my requests and he will give me peace. What a different approach to life! I want to learn this new way of dealing with my anxiety.

Father, thank you for being patient with me when I forget to come to you in my anxious moments.

Being confident of this very thing, that He who has begun a good work in you will complete it until the day of Jesus Christ.
—Phil. 1:6

All my life I felt so empty, alone, and unloved. For many years I tried to fill the emptiness with drugs, alcohol, food, and unhealthy relationships. My life was miserable until I cried out to God for help. He heard my cry and directed me to Remuda Ranch where my recovery began.

After I made the choice to live, I had to admit I was powerless and could not recover on my own. I found a real sense of strength in admitting that my eating disorder was controlling my life; I no longer had to pretend I had my life "together."

Recovery has been hard and painful; it is a challenge to find out who I really am! But the good work that God began in me is continuing. He has blessed me with people who love me, support me, and really understand.

I am finding that it takes time to break down all the walls of defense that I put up over the years. Accepting God's love makes me feel I'm worth making the effort to change.

Father, I thank you for giving me the strength and courage to get help! I trust you to finish the good work you have started.

"Honor your father and mother," which is the first commandment with promise: "that it may be well with you and you may live long on the earth."
—Eph. 6:2–3

My parents played a part in my choice to become eating-disordered. It has been hard not to blame them entirely for all the bad things in my life.

I have learned that hanging on to resentment toward my parents has only hurt me. I worked through my anger at my mom and dad for the hurts they caused, but to stay stuck in that anger would be costly. I am now trying to let go of my anger toward my parents.

It is hard to get past being angry at them, but I have to face my responsibility. I can choose to remain unhealthy, blaming my parents for the way I am, or I can make new choices for my life. There comes a time when I can no longer blame my past, as ugly as it is, for my present condition.

Today I am a parent, and I am painfully aware of how easy it is to make mistakes with children! This perspective helps me give my parents a degree of honor for the job they did parenting me, even though it was not perfect.

Lord, I ask that you guide me in my parenting and help me to forgive my parents for their mistakes.

August 12 – PERSEVERANCE IS REWARDED

*So do not throw away your confidence; it will be
richly rewarded. You need to persevere so that
when you have done the will of God, you will
receive what he has promised.*
—Heb. 10:35–36 NIV

This verse was given to me by a dear friend while I
was in treatment for my eating disorder. At that time
my confidence was wavering. I was starting to wonder
if I could make it through the program.

The realization that abstinence alone would not
guarantee wholeness was terrifying! I could not imagine going home and surviving in the very same set of
circumstances that propelled me into treatment.

This friend saw my progress and abilities more
clearly than I could. With her encouragement I began
to realize that I was strong enough to persevere! Many
times that has meant just holding my ground and not
getting sidetracked.

I have held my ground; I have reversed setbacks!
With God's power I am well on my way to recovery. I
am reaping the rewards of becoming healthy; my life is
now rich and full.

Allow yourself to be encouraged. It helps to spend
time with friends who can help you see yourself more
clearly. Help others in that same way!

Thank you, Father, for your Word and for encouraging friends.

And do not be conformed to this world, but be transformed by the renewing of your mind.

—Rom. 12:2

I spent the better part of my life conforming myself to the world's image of beauty. I was determined to attain a perfect body. My quest consumed me; I was willing to sacrifice both health and relationships to reach this ideal.

Finally there came a point where the price was too high! My body was breaking down; sometimes my heart pounded so hard that I thought it would jump right out of my chest. My relationships, like my body, were also breaking down; I was overwhelmed with loneliness.

This world tells me that beauty is on the outside, but have you noticed how the standard for beauty changes from year to year? God looks at my inner beauty, and what he desires does not change. In his eyes, I am a beautiful part of his creation.

How can I be transformed instead of conformed to this world? The change comes from renewing my mind. In today's lingo, I must change my "self-talk." When I look in a mirror, I no longer say, "I'm fat and ugly!" Instead I say, "I am fearfully and wonderfully made" (Ps. 139:14). When I make a mistake, I no longer believe that I *am* a mistake. If God loves me, cellulite and all, who am I to say he's wrong?

Father, teach me to see the beauty that you see in me.

*And the rain descended, the floods came, and the
winds blew and beat on that house; and it did not
fall, for it was founded on the rock. And the rain
descended, the floods came, and the winds beat on
that house; and it fell. And great was its fall.*
—Matt. 7:25, 27

As a child, I loved to sing a song in Sunday school
about this passage of Scripture. The song has hand motions and describes in detail how each house was built,
and how the storms came and blew. It was always such
fun to end the song by hollering, "Smash!"

I have enjoyed teaching that song to my own children and those I teach in Sunday school. It brings back
the child in me; it is hard to refrain from acting out the
motions playfully.

The words of the song have almost lost their meaning for me because I have sung them so many times.
The message is clear: things built on a firm foundation
stand against the storms, but things built on shaky
ground fall apart under pressure.

My life was built on unstable ground. Although I pro-
fessed to be a follower of Christ, my faith in him was
weak. I really worshipped the gods of beauty, riches,
and perfection, none of which provided a solid foundation for my life. Today I am rebuilding my life on the
solid rock of Jesus. He has provided me with the
strength to withstand the storms of life.

Lord, please remind me when I am on shaky ground.

Blessed are you who weep now, for you shall laugh.
—Luke 6:21

In the year since I entered treatment for my eating disorder, I think I have cried more than I ever had before in twenty-eight years of life. There have been times when I cried for hours, even days! I cry for the sadness and pain in my childhood; there are many painful memories that I never grieved. I feel better after I let the tears flow.

I once thought that by pushing painful memories down inside me with food they would somehow go away. That was not the case. When I think of all the years of my life that I have invested in my eating disorder, it makes me cry.

Recently I became acutely aware of the ways I hurt others with my selfishness. I cry when I think of how my children have suffered because I am not whole. I share my tears with them, and I let them know that I am sorry for the pain I have caused.

Getting in touch with the pain and sadness in my life has not been all bad. Because I am learning to acknowledge my feelings of sadness, other feelings are coming to the surface as well. Going through suffering has made me more aware of real joy. At times I believed I would never smile or laugh again, but I have, and it feels good!

Lord, I trust that the crying will not last forever.

> *Whenever I am afraid,*
> *I will trust in You.*
> —Ps. 56:3

For years a thick wall of fear surrounded me like a cloud. I was afraid of failure and of new people and new situations. I was terrified that others could see me as the miserable failure that I thought I was. The fear became so overwhelming that it paralyzed me emotionally.

My self-esteem was based on what I looked like, so when I thought I did not look good enough I hid myself. Much of the time I isolated myself from my friends and family. I dreaded going to my husband's company dinner, and I starved myself for days before the event. If I did not believe that I had lost enough weight, I would come up with an excuse not to go. Eating in front of new people was too great a fear. I thought everyone would look at me and think, "How can that fat pig eat?"

In recovery I am learning to turn to God with my fears. When I am confronted with an uncomfortable situation and I'm tempted to run away, turning to God gives me the courage to face things head on.

God knows my fears! I can tell him my secrets and trust that he will understand. My feelings are not silly or inconsequential to God; I am his child.

Heavenly Father, help me to trust you with more of my fears each day.

Dear Lord,

Sometimes I wonder if I am even capable of trusting you. When the slightest problem arises I begin to doubt that you will take care of me. I question you and I worry about my lack of faith.

I know you have never led me astray; many of my problems are due to my own poor choices. I start pretending that I can recover on my own, and then— watch out! I find myself in big trouble.

Lord, it is so easy to forget that you were there in my darkest hour. Through seven years of bulimia, you protected my life. You directed me to a place where it was safe to share my secrets and begin the process of healing. I know you are guiding me during my time in treatment, Father.

Lord, thank you for this new start. This path of recovery is rougher than I anticipated, but I will trust you to be by my side. I am excited about this new life, one without the constant thoughts of food and self. Teach me to accept love and happiness.

I will continue to rest in your loving arms! Please forgive me when I forget to rely on you. Thank you for saving me from the awful pain of my eating disorder. Amen.

I will praise You, for I am fearfully and wonderfully made.
                                        —Ps. 139:14

For years, I believed ninety-nine percent of the Bible. I totally accepted almost all of God's Word, no questions asked. But part of the Scriptures gave me trouble.

I choked on the verses in the Bible that dealt with God creating me. I did not believe that I was wonderfully made, although I certainly had no trouble accepting that truth for others.

Because I believe the Bible is true, I had to find a way around those particular passages. My answer was to apply them to my soul, my inner self. I could believe that my mind is a wonderful creation, and I accepted that God skillfully wrought my sense of humor.

The truth is that God created me to be me! Not only did he create my soul and spirit, God fashioned my body as well. He gave me an overabundance of hips and short legs, but he also gave me beautiful eyes and curves in all the right places.

When I look in the mirror and am tempted to despise the creation, I acknowledge what my Creator has done. I learned that I cannot love God and yet hate his creation. I will praise him for his work!

Lord, teach me to praise you when I look in the mirror.

Commit your way to the LORD,
Trust also in Him,
And He shall bring it to pass.
        —Ps. 37:5

One morning as I was journaling I glanced up at my calendar on the wall. In the early stages of my recovery, I kept track of my abstinence. I marked the days with an O when I had abstained from disordered eating behaviors. On the days when I binged and purged, I made an X.

The last three days on the calendar had an X in each square. My first thought was, "Strike three, you're out!" At that moment I had a choice to make. I could walk off the field of recovery, or I could try again.

I decided not to quit, and my recovery has progressed because of that choice. Actually recovery from addiction is no game. Three strikes simply means it is time for a new start. God willingly gives second chances, and third and fourth chances, too!

I have committed myself and my recovery to God. I am trusting him to bring about the healing that is necessary in my life.

_____

Lord, thank you for the chance at a new start.

Be still, and know that I am God.
—Ps. 46:10

Quiet time, rest, and relaxation are foreign terms to me! I fear that if I slow down I might gain weight; nothing could be worse. So I keep myself moving all the time to keep the calories burning!

I believe there are deeper reasons why I will not slow down. If I slow down long enough, I might have to think about what is inside me. I do not want to face the fear and pain. What will I find if I take time to look inside my heart?

I fear spending time with God, because I'm afraid I will learn that he does not truly love me. Deep inside me there is a fear that I am unlovable. To keep from facing that fear I keep myself busy, with no time to think or feel.

Many times I sensed God whispering, "Be still and know me." What does it mean to know he is God? For me it means learning about God and his attributes. When I truly know God as he is, I am able to rest in the knowledge that he is in control.

———————

Dear Lord, help me to slow down long enough to really know you.

But may the God of all grace, who called us to
His eternal glory by Christ Jesus, after you have
suffered a while, perfect, establish, strengthen,
and settle you.   —1 Peter 5:10

It is such a comfort to know that God is involved in my life. Somehow I just can't picture God sitting passively in heaven, watching life go by on earth.

God is interested in the hard times, sufferings, and struggles as well as the good times. In his loving way God gave me the gift of his Holy Spirit to be near me. I sense his presence offering strength, comfort, and guidance as I make my way through life.

As my daughter learned to walk, I stayed close to her. Each time she fell I picked her up and made sure she was steady on her feet before allowing her to try again. I could not prevent her from falling, but I could be there to make sure she was safe.

I know that God is the best parent around! As I stumble and fall over the bumps in my life, he is there to pick me up. He allows me to fall; that's just part of learning to walk. But he is always there to make sure that my feet are planted before I take my next step.

Father, thank you for perfecting me through my suffering.

> *Is it nothing to you, all you who pass by?*
> *Behold and see*
> *If there is any sorrow like my sorrow.*
> —Lam. 1:12

Often I am so caught up in my own pain that it seems like no one else has been through as much as I have. When I allow myself to dwell on my circumstances, I fall into the trap of self-pity.

I have seen my share of pain. I have a history of both physical and sexual abuse. I attempted to numb myself from pain with food, but it didn't work! That only added another problem to my list.

A support group member recently requested furniture for a woman who had been released from jail. I am thankful that I never experienced that kind of pain! Hearing that announcement made me very aware of how many people are hurting.

My life has been far from perfect, but it could be worse! God has used the pain in my life to equip me to help others. He used my eating disorder to propel me into treatment; there I was given the tools I needed to live.

When I start feeling like I am the only one in the world who has seen trouble, all it takes is a quick look around me. There are plenty of folks who have not yet started to deal with their pain.

Lord, be with all those who are hurting, even me!

NO TURNING BACK – *August 23*

I know your works. See, I have set before you an
open door, and no one can shut it; for you have a
little strength, have kept My word, and have not
denied My name.
                              —Rev. 3:8

Do you ever wonder if recovery is really possible? God used this verse to encourage me about my own progress. He gave me hope that recovery is not only possible but also inevitable. God has opened the door to recovery for me, and no one can close it, not even me!

If I relapse, the door to recovery will still be open to me. God knows that I am not strong, and his strength has carried me through the tough times. I am also strengthened through friends, support groups, therapy, and my food plan.

Each day God gives me another chance! I wake up and choose to go through the door that he has opened for my healing. I draw on all the resources that our Lord has made available to me. The door will never close; all I need is the determination to walk through it and keep on recovering.

Father, please give me the courage and determination that I need
each day. May I never turn my back on the door to my recovery.

August 24 – DON'T BE DISCOURAGED

> *Look, the LORD your God has set the land before you; go up and possess it, as the LORD God of your fathers has spoken to you; do not fear or be discouraged.*
> —Deut. 1:21

When I got on the scales to weigh myself I was shocked to see I had gained a few pounds. During treatment for my eating disorder I had decided to keep my weight at a certain level; now I had gone over the limit.

All because of a few pounds I panicked. I allowed my feelings to take control, and I felt a mixture of anger, loneliness, and fear. I ran to the mirror and judged myself as fat and ugly. The thoughts of returning to old behaviors came to mind. I wanted to eat to numb myself from the feelings.

Instead I chose not to endanger my recovery. I see myself coping with feelings, learning to make good choices, and becoming more honest. The issues before me are painful, but I am encouraged by the growth I see.

God has provided me with an opportunity for healing; he has set before me the land of recovery. When I feel discouraged and afraid, I remind myself that he will give me strength.

Father, I thank you that I am now able to feel. Give me the courage I need to walk through my fears to the land of health.

*Do not let your adornment be merely outward—
arranging the hair, wearing gold, or putting on fine
apparel—rather let it be the hidden person of the
heart, with the incorruptible beauty of a gentle
and quiet spirit, which is very precious in the
sight of God.*
　　　　　　　　　　　　　—1 Peter 3:3–4

I used to spend at least ninety percent of my time thinking about food. I obsessed about calories constantly; every bite was accounted for. Much of the rest of my time was spent on the scale or in front of the mirror. I worried about how much I weighed and what I looked like.

I was fighting a losing battle! No matter how little I ate or how much weight I lost, it was never enough. The reflection in the mirror was never satisfactory.

When I read these verses I was so relieved! The pressure to look perfect was removed.

I must admit, though, that the change in thinking did not happen the first time I read the passage. I prayed that God would show me what was really important in life, which things would last. I prayed daily that God would give me a gentle and quiet spirit. As I prayed my priorities changed! I'm learning to put less importance on my looks and spend more time on things that matter.

Dear Father, remind me of these verses when my priorities get mixed up. Continue to teach me that what I look like is not most important.

A man who has friends must himself be friendly,
But there is a friend who sticks closer than a
brother.
—Prov. 18:24

During my recovery it has become painfully clear who my real friends are. A few people have stuck by me through all of my pain. They were there to support me while I still struggled with my eating disorder, and they encouraged me to seek help when I needed it.

Many other people have not been supportive of me in my quest for wholeness. Some are not able to deal with the changes that have taken place in my life.

I thank God for providing me with several good friends who love me no matter what. I have also learned to rely on him for many of my needs. It is a comfort to know that even if the people around me are not understanding, God understands.

He has given me the strength to do what is best for me and not depend on others' approval. I have learned that many of my friendships were based on unhealthy patterns. I am now making new friends who understand and support my recovery.

Father, thank you for your love and acceptance. I am grateful for loving friends.

But let patience have its perfect work, that you may
be perfect and complete, lacking nothing.
                                        —James 1:4

Perfection is my goal! I want to be whole, inside and out, but I am not very patient in the process.

These days I am less obsessed with becoming perfect on the outside, but I am still driven to become a better person. As I grow closer to God, I see more clearly how unlike him I am. I am lacking in many areas of personal growth.

God is much more patient with me than I am with myself. He does not have me on a rigid timetable; that is all my doing. I spent so many years numbed to life that I feel driven to make up for lost time. But I can't rewind my life like a videotape and do it over again.

I think God did give me a new start at life by allowing me to be in treatment at Remuda Ranch. There I was given the tools I need to live without my eating disorder. God is perfecting me; it is a slow, often painful process. He is gently peeling away the ugly layers of my heart so that I am becoming more and more like him. The least I can do is be patient.

Lord, thank you for working in my life. Teach me to be patient while you make me complete.

> *Finally, my brethren, be strong in the Lord and in the power of His might. Put on the whole armor of God, that you may be able to stand against the wiles of the devil.* —Eph. 6:10–11

When I stand in front of the mirror I am usually dissatisfied with the way I look. I have often thought, "I wish I had another body!"

I am working on changing such thinking. Telling myself "I am a flawless creation of God" feels a little awkward, but I am trying to reprogram my brain. Instead of dwelling on the imperfections in my appearance, I concentrate on what positive changes are taking place in my life.

I am learning to protect myself with God's Word each day before I dress. I visualize myself wearing a belt of God's truth, and a breastplate of righteousness. I picture the footgear of peace, and the shield of faith. It helps to remember that I am protected by God (Eph. 6:14–18).

When my thoughts turn sour because of the way I look, I remind myself that I am covered with a force field by my heavenly Father. He is teaching me to accept myself as he does.

Thank you, Lord, for the way you created me. Protect me during this stage of my recovery.

Indeed we count them blessed who endure. You have heard of the perseverance of Job and seen the end intended by the Lord—that the Lord is very compassionate and merciful.   —James 5:11

From my desk I watched as a man refinished the brass elevator. It was a painstakingly slow process! He patiently followed all the right steps, working on tiny areas at a time. For a while the elevator definitely looked worse!

I began to wonder if he really knew what he was doing. I wanted to jump up and give him some advice or give him a hand—I who knew nothing at all about brass!

It struck me that I do exactly the same thing with God. Although he knows much more than I do about the big picture of my life, I want to tell him what to do. I struggle not to push God out of the way and take over myself.

I am so impatient! God is working on little pieces of my life at a time. I want to take shortcuts and just get it all over with. Sometimes I don't like what I see, and I am concerned about the end result. I need to remember what that elevator looks like now. It is more beautiful and shiny than ever before.

Father, help me learn to trust you with the work of my life. Remind me that you know what's best about the pace and the outcome.

I will extol You, O LORD, for You have lifted me up,
And have not let my foes rejoice over me.

—Ps. 30:1

When I was in high school our football team was horrible. I think the team had only one victory during my senior year. The opponents looked forward to playing our school, because they were almost certain to win. The opposing team members tormented our players unmercifully!

In this game of life, I have often felt like the underdog. Sometimes it seems like I am being attacked from all sides, and I am losing badly.

When things get tough, my star player enters the field. God lifts me out of the depths of defeat and carries me toward victory! I am so thankful that my recovery from eating disorders is not dependent on my effort alone. God has provided me with a team that is able to support me. I have learned to rely on doctors, therapists, and support groups to help me win!

Father, help me remember that I don't have to play this game alone. Thank you for being part of my team.

For the LORD does not see as man sees; for man looks at the outward appearance, but the LORD looks at the heart.
—1 Sam. 16:7

In this verse the Lord told the prophet Samuel to anoint a new king, and he specifically instructed him not to judge by appearance or stature. God's tape measure for the future king was the condition of his heart.

The world judges people by their looks. I used to spend so much time and energy trying to perfect my appearance that I had little time left to tend to my inner being. The more time I spent working on my appearance and obsessing about my weight, the less time I had to spend with God. As a result I had a shallow, distant relationship with God.

For many years I yearned for acceptance, but I was unable to accept myself. Even worse, I rejected God's acceptance of me. I spent hours exercising my body and seeking approval for my looks, but I neglected to spend time with God. I firmed up my thighs while my faith grew flabby.

In the end it will not matter what I weigh or how I look. It is the state of my heart, not my body, that has eternal significance. I pray that when the Lord looks at my heart, he will be pleased with what he finds.

Lord, help me pour myself into becoming close to you.

Yesterday I saw only clouds above the sea.

They rolled and churned in anger as they closed in around me.

As the waves crashed in upon me, I fought for every breath, afraid if I quit struggling, it would surely mean my death.

So desperately I tried to swim against the fiercest tide.

My will was swiftly weakening, and I could feel my strength subside.

I struggled on in anguish, trying so hard to erase the pain of all the memories I didn't want to face.

All the strength I had was nothing when it was mine alone.

For love and peace could never thrive in a heart that's made of stone.

When I finally began going down for the last time, I cried out to God, and he put his hand in mine.

He heard my voice above the roar of wind, and waves, and storm.

As the sea poured out its fury, he held me in his arms.

He accepted me, just as I was, with all my guilt and shame, and lovingly assured me he had taken away the blame.

Although yesterday I saw only clouds above the stormy sea, today the sun broke through the clouds and brought new hope to me.

> *Though he fall, he shall not be utterly cast down;*
> *For the LORD upholds him with His hand.*
> —Ps. 37:24

I failed again! The dean of women called me into her office and gently recommended that I drop out of school for the rest of the semester. Just a few days earlier I had attempted suicide; she thought that I could deal with my problems better without the added stress of school.

I felt lost and the pain was more intense than ever before. I felt cut off from God, my friends, and my family. I was falling!

There, in the midst of my despair, I met Jesus. It was as if he reached out to hold me. For the first time in my life, I knew for sure that he loved me. The pain of the recovery process was still before me, but I was no longer alone. I continued to feel separated from my family and friends, but Jesus filled my heart.

Since then I have again felt like I was in danger of falling, but I have not feared being utterly cast down. I know the Lord is there; he holds me up!

Lord, please never let go of my hand.

> *"You shall march around the city, all you men of war; you shall go all around the city once. This you shall do six days. And seven priests shall bear seven trumpets of rams' horns before the ark. But the seventh day you shall march around the city seven times, and the priests shall blow the trumpets. It shall come to pass, when they make a long blast with the ram's horn, and when you hear the sound of the trumpet, that all the people shall shout with a great shout; then the wall of the city will fall down flat."*
>
> —Josh. 6:3–5

In order to conquer a city, God instructed Joshua to have his people march around Jericho blowing horns and shouting. It does not make much sense to me, and I can imagine that Joshua was scratching his head over the plan, too! But guess what? It worked.

I am recovering from anorexia, bulimia, and compulsive overeating. At times I have not been too sure that the plan God gave me would work. A lot of my recovery program does not make sense to me. I would not have thought that going to groups and therapy would be the answer to my problem, but guess what? It's working! God is working through many things to bring about healing in my life.

Father, help me to do what I need to do.

> *And you will seek Me and find Me, when you*
> *search for Me with all your heart. I will be found*
> *by you, says the LORD, and I will bring you back*
> *from your captivity.*
> —Jer. 29:13–14

I find such comfort in knowing that all I have to do to find God is to seek him with my heart! The Creator of the universe is not hiding from me. He is available to me when I search for him.

When things are out of control and I feel all alone, I have learned to look to God for my strength. I cry out to him and he gives me peace.

For years I was held captive by eating disorders. I could not break free from the addiction on my own. Fortunately, God is drawing me out of that prison now; I am no longer bound to my compulsion with food.

What is holding you captive? If you truly seek God with your heart, he can bring you back. My God is more powerful than the emotional ties of a devastating past! He is freeing me from the strangling hold my eating disorder had over my life.

I thank you, Lord, for making yourself available to me when I look for you. I am so grateful that I am no longer held captive by eating disorders.

"Can anyone hide himself in secret places,
So I shall not see him?" says the LORD;
"Do I not fill heaven and earth?" says the LORD.
—Jer. 23:24

At one point in my stay at the treatment center I was afraid of everything around me. I saw a mouse and it bothered me for days. I hated walking to my room at night; I dreaded going into the dark. I personalized every situation until I convinced myself that the center was not a safe place to be.

I allowed the fears to take over to such a degree that I wanted to leave! I complained that because I did not feel safe, I couldn't be expected to continue my treatment. As I was sharing my thoughts and feelings in a group session, I realized that my fears were misplaced; I was really afraid of myself.

One night I let my fears overwhelm me. I badly wanted to run away, but I feared the consequences. I hid myself in the corner of my room between the bed and the wall. I could hear the staff calling my name and searching for me, but I kept quiet.

After I was found I admitted my fears and shared my pain with others. The staff and residents encouraged me to stay and walk through the fear of facing myself.

Even in that dark corner of my room I could not hide myself from God. He is everywhere!

Father, I know you see me when I'm hiding! Help me feel safe enough to come out and face you.

> *I can do all things through Christ who strengthens me.*
>
> —Phil. 4:13

I have always loved this verse, and I really believe it with all of my heart. I used to think it only applied to the big events in life, like taking major exams and having babies.

"All" means just that—everything! So I decided to take this verse at its word. I wondered if Christ would give me the strength I needed to eat. Could God help me survive a stay in a treatment center for my eating disorder?

During the months I spent at Remuda Ranch, I asked God to show himself to me in very practical ways. Mealtime had always been difficult for me. I made a card to place in front of me during meals. On it I wrote, "I can eat this meal through him who gives me strength." Eating was still not enjoyable, but God did give me the strength to complete each meal!

I have found that he really does give me the strength to do everything in my life. I have learned that God is beside me, even during the daily struggles I face.

Lord, with you I can do all things!

Therefore be imitators of God as dear children.
—Eph. 5:1

For most of my life I have tried to pattern myself after the people around me. As a little girl I loved to be with my Aunt Teri. I loved to follow her around as she cooked and sewed, and I wanted to grow up to be just like her.

Years later I tried to copy the styles of women I saw on television. I wanted my clothes and body to look just like the beautiful models. The trouble is, I am not shaped like the tall, thin women in the shows and advertisements. I constantly felt frustrated because I could not make myself look like they did. One factor that led to my eating disorder was the belief that my body was unacceptable because it did not look the way I thought it should.

I often find myself imitating the laugh of a friend or trying to do my hair just like a style that I find attractive. I have realized that I am trying to find acceptance and approval by imitating others.

God wants me to copy him! He desires that I mimic him in my thoughts and behavior. I am learning to pattern myself after him.

Father, teach me to follow you. You are worth copying.

> *For by You I can run against a troop,*
> *By my God I can leap over a wall.*
> —Ps. 18:29

In my recovery, I came up against many walls. I would progress steadily and then suddenly come to a standstill.

Part of my eating disorder was my unwillingness to face things head on. When an issue appeared overwhelming, my tendency was to retreat for a time, hoping the problem would disappear. I would cry, "This is too hard; I'm afraid!" My avoidance only prolonged the inevitable. The issues did not go away.

My strength was not enough to hurdle the walls of fear. I learned that my faith in God would see me through whatever life brought my way. God's strength helped me face the things I was trying so hard to avoid.

God's presence did not eliminate the fear or take away the pain, but by my God I have lived to recover from my eating disorder!

Heavenly Father, grab hold of my hand and take me over the walls.

*The LORD will command His lovingkindness
    in the daytime,
And in the night His song shall be with me—
A prayer to the God of my life.* —Ps. 42:8

During the darkest period of my eating disorder, the nights were full of terror for me. After everyone had gone to bed I found it impossible to sleep. My deep fears grew as the house became quiet.

I tried drowning out the fears with television. Filling myself with food did no good. I tried to rid myself of the fears by purging, but still I was overwhelmed by them.

Each night I feared falling asleep. What if I died in the night? I was terrified that God would find me unacceptable. The nights were truly a nightmare!

Occasionally, I would try reading the Bible and praying, but God felt far away. As I read his Word, my guilt grew and I felt more condemned.

At the end of my rope, I was faced with two choices: suicide or life. I stopped trying to run from my inner turmoil and ran to God instead. He offered me peace and contentment.

The Bible no longer condemns me; I find hope there. I stopped stuffing my fears and pain with food and started feasting on God's Word. I no longer dread nighttime, because his song is with me.

Lord, thank you for the quiet nights. I love to hear you singing to me.

> *Charm is deceitful and beauty is passing,*
> *But a woman who fears the LORD,*
> *   she shall be praised.*   —Prov. 31:30

In this verse the writer describes the qualities of an excellent woman. She has many talents, like planting vineyards and making clothes for her family. Nowhere does it mention her looks! This lady sounds like Superwoman, but beauty, a firm body, or thinness doesn't count toward her worth.

This passage reminds me that beauty is passing; it just doesn't last. The quality that God finds attractive in women is reverence for him. My relationship with God sets me apart in a crowd much more than the way I look.

My priorities were all backward for most of my life! I did not think fearing God was as important as my outward beauty. My self-esteem was based entirely on how I looked. As I spent more and more time focusing on my body, my relationship with God grew shallow.

The Lord in his mercy showed me the error in my thinking. I have found that the closer I get to him, the less obsessed I become with my looks.

_____

Thank you, Lord, for showing me what is important to you. Help me become an excellent woman.

Finding out what is acceptable to the Lord.
—Eph. 5:10

The God I grew up with was harsh and unloving. I lived in fear of doing things that were not pleasing to him, and I was extremely guilt-ridden.

Many of the rules that were enforced in our home were attributed to "what God would want us to do." I have since learned that God would not have been pleased with many of the things that went on in our home.

I blindly accepted my parents' view of God and the Bible without finding out for myself what was true. I accepted my parents' words as gospel; I held them in high esteem and never thought to question them.

My performance never seemed to be good enough for my parents, and I assumed God was not pleased either. No matter how hard I tried I did not feel accepted. This is one factor that led to my eating disorder.

Today I am earnestly seeking to know what is truly acceptable to God; I want to understand what he expects of me. I do not want to live under an unnecessary burden of guilt and shame.

I have learned that nothing I can do can make me acceptable to God. On my own I can struggle and strive to gain his approval without achieving it. My relationship with Jesus is what makes me acceptable to God. What a relief!

Father, thank you for accepting me; please free me from the need to perform to gain your love.

> *Be kindly affectionate to one another with brotherly*
> *love, in honor giving preference to one another.*
> —Rom. 12:10

It's hard for me to find a balance between behaving like a doormat and expecting everyone to bow to my wishes. I have learned that I allowed myself to be victimized many times in my life.

Lately, I think I have overcorrected for playing the role of the victim; now I don't want to do anything that doesn't suit me perfectly. Where's the middle ground? I do not want to live life on either end of that pendulum.

Christ knew his own worth and value. His position as Son of God gave him the power to control the universe. But he did not lord his strength over others. He was secure in his identity, so he was able to face ridicule and rebukes without changing how he felt about himself.

I will have to do things in life that I do not want to do. For instance, some people in authority rub me the wrong way. I struggle to follow directions because I fear being victimized again. Still, I am learning who I am in God's eyes. With that knowledge I am able to submit to authority without feeling like I am worthless.

Father, help me learn how to cooperate with others without discarding my own thoughts and feelings.

*We were burdened beyond measure, above strength,
so that we despaired even of life. Yes, we had the
sentence of death in ourselves, that we should not
trust in ourselves but in God who raises the dead,
who delivered us from so great a death, and does
deliver us; in whom we trust that He will still
deliver us.*
　　　　　　　　　　　　　　—2 Cor. 1:8–10

I had already been away from my family for three months in a treatment center for anorexia. Now my therapist wanted me to stay another two to three months! My heart sank. In fact, what he said to me seemed like a death sentence.

My family was brokenhearted to think of an even longer separation. To encourage me my husband sent me this verse. After the initial shock I realized that I could let the decision hinder my progress or I could search for God in the situation. I decided to try to discover what he wanted me to learn while I was still away from home.

God proved to be so faithful! It was still painful to be away from my family, but he was my comfort and delivered me from my distress. My relationship with God grew stronger as I had to rely on him to be my strength.

————————————

*Thank you, Lord, for using the pressures of life to cause me to rely on
you. Please deliver me.*

> *A fool's mouth is his destruction,*
> *And his lips are the snare of his soul.*
> —Prov. 18:7

I really thought I had come clean with all my secrets. After admitting that I had an eating disorder and entering treatment, I did not think anything was still hidden. I was wrong!

I remember feeling really sorry for many women who were in treatment with me. Their relationships with men were horrible; many had abusive, destructive marriages. I did not want to admit that I had attracted the same kind of man.

Part of the problem was denial; I did not want to look at reality. I was also too prideful to admit another failure in my life. Shame also played a part; I couldn't believe that my husband's problems are not all my fault.

Foolishly I had kept up the facade. Everyone thought that he was such a good man. None of their husbands helped with the house and the kids. Their admiration only fed my secret.

Admitting that my husband is not Prince Charming has been extremely painful. Now I am trying to make sure that there are no more secrets.

Lord, please keep me from being foolish.

> *When Jesus heard that, He said to them, "Those
> who are well have no need of a physician, but
> those who are sick."*
> —Matt. 9:12

Seeing therapists and psychiatrists is hard because it means I still need help. I keep thinking that I can recover all alone.

Several times since I left treatment, I decided to take matters into my own hands. Mental health care is costly, and I hated to pay for the prescriptions I need to stay on an even keel.

One day I decided that I no longer needed to take my prescription for anxiety. After all, I had many months of abstinence under my belt. I should be able to handle stress by now, right? Although the doctor had given me a plan for weaning myself off the drug, I knew better.

I stopped the drug cold turkey and almost ruined my recovery in the process. For one week my body was in shock. My face broke out, I couldn't sleep, and I woke up in the middle of the night throwing up. I was exhausted and irritable, but I remained stubborn and inflexible.

In the end, my emotions paid the price. I became depressed and suicidal.

Now I know that part of my recovery is following a plan designed by others who are rational and objective about my needs.

Father, teach me to trust you to guide my doctors.

September 16 – WALKING ON THE WATER

*So He said, "Come." And when Peter had come
down out of the boat, he walked on the water to
go to Jesus. But when he saw that the wind was
boisterous, he was afraid; and beginning to
sink he cried out, saying, "Lord, save me!"*
                                              —Matt. 14:29–30

Recovery has been like the storm-tossed waters. My
goal, to become healthy, is on the other side, and the
only way to get there is to get out of the boat and walk
on the water.

As long as I keep looking to Jesus I won't slip. If I
start looking at the size of the waves (my pain), I become overwhelmed and I sink.

I can choose to stay in the safety of the boat (my
eating disorder), but those gale-force winds are tearing
it to bits, and it's going down. I am confronted with a
decision: do I go down with the ship, or do I step out in
faith onto the water?

I could wait to see if the storm will pass before I step
out, but I know in my heart that the storm only grows
worse. So, I step out into the angry tide and try to keep
my eyes on Jesus as I walk across the sea of recovery.
When I am tempted to return to the security of the
ship, when I fear that the wind will knock me over,
when the sea of pain threatens to swallow me up, I will
call out to the Lord. He will save me.

Lord, help me keep my eyes on you as you lead me across the water.

For do I now persuade men, or God? Or do I seek to please men? For if I still pleased men, I would not be a bondservant of Christ. —Gal. 1:10

Developing and maintaining relationships is a special challenge for me during this time of recovery. Having honest interchanges with people is next to impossible while I am in the grips of anorexia.

I always saw myself as being blank, devoid of any personal preferences. Usually I went along with others in order to gain their approval. I felt lacking in inner substance.

In order to satisfy the image others have had of me, I constantly tried to outguess them so I could be what I thought they expected of me. I resented the very people I tried to please, but I was fearful of expressing my true feelings. I was afraid of being rejected.

Realizing my true worth in Christ has given me new hope for change! I no longer have to be the world's doormat. Believing that I am fully loved and accepted by God gives me security.

When I seek God's approval I feel less threatened by others. As I relax and allow my defenses to come down I can begin to experience healthy, loving relationships.

Father, help me to seek your approval and stop trying to please others.

> *Trust in Him at all times, you people;*
> *Pour out your heart before Him;*
> *God is a refuge for us.* —Ps. 62:8

Sometimes my road to recovery seems too rough! It is so painful that I almost believe I am walking on broken glass with bare feet.

I am still tempted to use food to numb the pain. For years food was my refuge. I filled my stomach to comfort myself, and then I purged my feelings of guilt, anger, depression, and loneliness in the toilet. When I purged the food, I was really longing to pour out my heart to someone who would understand and not think I was crazy.

Now I have the confidence that God listens and understands. I trust him most of the time, but there are still times when my life feels out of control. It is hard to trust someone I cannot see. At these times I find myself wanting to take refuge in my old friend, food.

God is worthy of my trust at all times, even when things are out of control. He is my refuge, the Rock that shelters me from the storm. When the road gets rough, I no longer run to the refrigerator; I run to him. God waits for me with open arms and a loving heart.

Lord, thank you for being my refuge. I want to turn only to you in times of trouble.

But indeed for this purpose I have raised you up,
that I may show My power in you, and that My
name may be declared in all the earth.
—Ex. 9:16

As a youngster I watched our neighbor as he worked on his model T. The car was in mint condition, and he spent hours each day waxing and polishing the exterior. This man sacrificed much of his time to assure that the chrome was shined and the car looked perfect.

It was a surprise to me to learn that the vehicle was lacking in one important area: it had no engine! I remember thinking how silly it was to spend all that time making the car look so good when it served no purpose. The function of the car was to be driven, but no matter how great it looked it could not fulfill its purpose.

My function in life is to show God's power! Through my abilities and actions his name can be glorified. It hurts me to acknowledge this, but I do not always fulfill my design. I behave as if I was created solely to look good on the outside.

Much of my time is spent in front of the mirror, making sure that everything on the outside is in mint condition. Now I want to concern myself with doing what I was created to do.

———————

Lord, thank you for reminding me how futile my efforts are to achieve a perfect appearance.

Little children, keep yourselves from idols.
—1 John 5:21

During treatment for my eating disorder I realized that I had very unrealistic expectations for life. I looked for answers in the wrong places. All my life I believed, "If only . . . then I would be happy!"

I eventually realized that none of the things I had put my faith in could make my life pain-free. I met women with lots of money who had the same problems I faced. Women whose bodies I envied were still empty and hurting.

I worked hard to let go of my distorted thinking; I wanted to learn to be content inside, not look to external things for happiness.

One last idol remained, however—the idol of abstinence. I accepted the fact that neither money nor a firm body could make me feel better about myself, but I held on to the delusion that if I were free from my eating disorder my life would be perfect.

It has been almost one year since I last binged and purged. My life is not perfect; I still have pain. I am very grateful for my new-found freedom from compulsion with food; I am convinced that I would not be alive today without it.

Abstinence in and of itself is not the answer to all of my problems. However, abstaining from bingeing and purging has allowed me to look closely at my pain and deal with it rationally.

Father, forgive me for worshipping abstinence.

"I am the vine, you are the branches. He who abides in Me, and I in him, bears much fruit; for without Me you can do nothing."
—John 15:5

During the thirteen-year period when I struggled with eating disorders, I tried many different things to get my eating under control. There was always some new gimmick that caught my eye.

The topic of one support group meeting was our futile attempts to fix ourselves. We all laughed as we shared the many different plans and gadgets that had been part of our efforts. At the time I thought it was funny, but when I think of it now I feel sad.

It is not humorous to think of all the time and money I wasted on diet programs and weight-loss tools. It breaks my heart to think of others who are hurting and desperate to fill their emptiness.

Just controlling my eating was not the answer to my pain. The outward behaviors were just a signal of deeper trouble. My "eating problem" was an eating disorder, and that is a serious thing!

After I had exhausted all my own ideas and had run out of hope, I finally decided to turn to God for help. I was unable to make a dent in the turmoil in my life without him. My relationship with him is a constant source of strength and hope as I continue on my journey to health.

Father, help me stay rooted in you.

> *Be kindly affectionate to one another with brotherly love, in honor giving preference to one another.*
> —Rom. 12:10

God has put in my heart a strong desire to help others. I have learned a lot from my own struggles that I want to share with hurting people. Many of the jobs I've done have prepared me to deal with all kinds of individuals.

I have prayed that the Lord would find a place where I could be used, and my prayers have been answered! Recently I learned of a position where all my talents and experience could be put to use. God used a friend to direct me to the place he has prepared for me.

My heart is full of anticipation as I begin this new venture! I want to bring hope to those who are in pain. It helps to give meaning to the agony I have endured.

My desire is to do the job that God has given me. I want others to know that there is "light at the end of the tunnel." By sharing myself, my fears and my own growth, I hope to encourage others who have been in the dark for so many years.

Lord, you have been my strength and inspiration. Please give me understanding for others.

When I was a child, I spoke as a child, I
understood as a child, I thought as a child; but
when I became a man, I put away childish things.
—1 Cor. 13:11

My childhood was tough. I was lonely and had little support. I was also abused, sexually and physically. I was on my own when I was sad or frightened. Needless to say, many of my needs went unmet.

With childish understanding, I developed manipulative ways of getting what I needed. I begged for attention by being a clown and a troublemaker. I made up stories so my friends would like me. I lied to my parents to get what I needed from them.

As an adult I continued to practice childish ways of getting my needs met. What had been survival tactics as a child did not work well as an adult. Controlling, manipulating, lying, and clowning alienated people. My eating disorder was my ultimate attempt to protect myself from the harsh world.

I'm ready to put away my childish thoughts, words, and thinking. God is teaching me new ways of being fulfilled. Best of all, I am teaching my children to ask me for what they need.

Lord Jesus, thank you for teaching me how to grow up! Help me to be like a child in faith but an adult in understanding.

> *He heals the brokenhearted*
> *And binds up their wounds.*
> —Ps. 147:3

Today my heart feels torn apart! I am grieving over hurts that others have caused me as well as pain I have inflicted on myself. All at once, the pain seems too great to bear.

I remember entering treatment and not feeling worthy of having an eating disorder. I wasn't sure that enough bad things had happened in my lifetime to qualify me for anorexia, bulimia, and compulsive overeating. When I heard other women's stories, I felt like I didn't deserve to be sick.

I learned that I had been burying years of hurts with food. I had hidden some horrible memories in the corners of my mind. As I opened myself up to the memories my heart began to break. Sometimes I still cannot believe that my memories of physical and sexual abuse are accurate!

As I have faced the pain, a little at a time, God is slowly healing my broken heart. I sense him beside me when the memories threaten to overwhelm me. God's peace has protected me from myself when I wanted to die.

I have learned that I tend to head for the refrigerator when I face pain. The food does not take the hurt away, but God can touch the open wounds in my heart if I allow him to.

God, please help me live through this pain.

But I want you to know, brethren, that the things which happened to me have actually turned out for the furtherance of the gospel. —Phil. 1:12

At times the circumstances of my life seem to imprison me. I wonder what I could have done to deserve all of this. My friend often says, "It's a good thing we don't get what we deserve!"

I allow my self-centeredness to alter the reality of my life. Without much effort I am able to blow things completely out of proportion to the actual situation. I forget that God can use my reaction to life's events as a witness of his work in me.

Paul's attitude during his imprisonment amazes me. He instilled courage in the early Christians. As they viewed his faith in God amid desperate circumstances, many gained strength.

When I think of Paul's life and the situations he had to face, I marvel at his devotion and faith. His attitude in prison motivates me to check my own response to life's trials.

Is it possible to show God's strength and power even in the middle of my recovery? Is my attitude one that is encouraging to others, even while I am in pain? I want people to see God's love in me. I don't have to be "all better" before I break free of the prison of negative, sour thinking.

Lord, give me wisdom to see myself clearly. I want others to see you through me.

> *"But behold, the hand of My betrayer is with Me on the table."*
> —Luke 22:21

It hurts so much to be betrayed by those closest to me! I am never prepared when people who love me hurt me deeply.

Today a good friend betrayed my confidence by telling someone else a secret that I had shared with her. I am deeply wounded. My reaction is to pull back from all those around me and retreat into myself. That's a very scary place to be when I'm hurting this badly.

The refrigerator is beckoning to me. All the food in there seems very appealing; I would like to drown out the pain with a ton of food. I know that's not the answer, though. Fortunately, I have been given new tools with which to deal with life. I know that even if I choose to abuse food, the pain will still be there.

I am making the choice to write about my feelings. I'm not sure why, but writing always helps me put things in perspective. I will call a friend and talk about my pain, and maybe I'll even cry. I choose not to put myself in a spot where I might endanger my recovery and my life.

Jesus understands my pain. He was betrayed by someone close to him; his friends denied they even knew him! He is a friend who will never hurt me.

Jesus, please keep me safe during this time of pain.

To everything there is a season,
A time for every purpose under heaven.
—Eccl. 3:1

I am so afraid of what lies ahead and what lies inside me. My time has come for the very thing I have prayed for, but the thing I fear the most.

It is time to give up my eating disorder. The abstinence will reveal deep hurts I never even knew were there. Yet I have to step out, reach out, let go. I must trust God enough to carry me through. If I choose to hang on, for even one more day, I will die before I taste what life can be.

I do not want to be another lost soul paralyzed by fear. The hardest part of recovery is staring me in the face: looking inside myself and facing what is there. Within me is a frightened little child whose shame is great.

Tonight is the first time I will sleep without a cookie in my hand or my head in the toilet. If I awaken overwhelmed by fear, I will do whatever it takes to keep from bingeing or purging.

Father, today is the day of a much-needed rainstorm; my roots will grow into something they never dreamed they could be.

Unless Your law had been my delight,
I would then have perished in my affliction.
—Ps. 119:92

God's Word became important to me while I was in treatment for anorexia. I learned to depend on it more than I ever had in my life. The Bible became my dearest companion.

Each day God opened my eyes to something new and exciting! All this happened while I struggled through the intense pain of my past and worked to overcome my eating disorder.

I felt a real sense of loss as I let go of the habits that had filled my life for so many years. I needed something new to fill that void inside me.

God has taken the place of anorexia in my life. Instead of focusing on my body and controlling my food intake, I have learned to turn to God. He has become my faithful friend and my constant companion.

Had it not been for my precious relationship with God, I am sure I would have perished in my affliction.

Lord, thank you for your Word that keeps me from perishing.

Then all who heard were amazed.
—Acts 9:21

When I read the account of Paul's transformation in the ninth chapter of Acts, I am amazed. One day he was killing the Christians, and the next day he had become one of them.

I'm sure this was an adjustment for Paul as well as for those around him. He was no longer persecuting those who loved Christ, so he didn't fit in with his old friends. On the other hand, the Christians remembered him for his brutality. I can imagine they had a hard time accepting him into their ranks.

I have had friends tell me, "You're different; I don't feel like I know you anymore." People around me are struggling to accept the new me. I am different!

The games I used to play are not part of me any longer; I try not to be a people-pleaser all the time. I used to do and give to gain acceptance. Now I am learning that my worth does not depend on what I do, but who I am.

The friends I used to eat with are not comfortable with me these days. I don't like food to be the central focus of every activity. My abstinence is intimidating to people who are still using food to numb their pain.

I know Paul was convinced that he had made the right choice, just as I have. I will not return to my old sick ways just to feel accepted.

Lord, stay close as I go through this time of change!

> *He delights in unchanging love.*
> —Mic. 7:18 NAS

I grew up thinking of God's love as being conditional upon my performance. I believed that if I lied he would not love me anymore. I thought God would love me only if I behaved perfectly.

Perfection has eluded me over the years; it seemed like I was anything but perfect most of the time. I believed that the less perfect I was, the less God could love me.

I grew more and more depressed as I struggled to win God's love. At one point my despair was so great that I actually tried to take my own life. At that moment I cried out to God to save me.

Changing my beliefs about God has been extremely difficult; I still find myself performing to gain his favor. To combat the lies I believed about God, I began immersing myself in Scriptures that taught about God's love and his mercy toward me. I let the words wash over me: "Love covers all sins" (Prov. 10:12b). "Yes, I have loved you with an everlasting love" (Jer. 31:3). "His merciful kindness is great toward us" (Ps. 117:2).

God's love toward me is everlasting, it doesn't change, and it covers all my sins!

Thank you, dear Father, for love that never runs dry.

I am reaching Lord—
my hand is open
can't you see?
I am reaching out to know you.

I am reaching Lord—
my heart is open
can't you see?
I am reaching out to know you.

I am reaching Lord—
can't you see?
Even though it frightens me,
I am reaching out to know you.

I was searching Lord,
Your hand I didn't see.
Yet through all my doubts and fears,
you were reaching out to me.

> *But his wife looked back behind him, and she*
> *became a pillar of salt.*
> —Gen. 19:26

Often I try to work my recovery with the plan God gave me while hanging on to my own ideas on how to get well. It is dangerous to walk forward and keep looking back at the same time; it just does not work very well.

The story of Lot's wife in the Old Testament describes what happened to one woman who would not let go of the past. She longed to stay where she felt comfortable, in old familiar surroundings. The cost was her life!

I have been given a new start, and I am grateful for that. At the same time I often wish for the old ways. Recovery is difficult, and often I wonder if it wasn't easier being controlled by my eating disorder. My memory can be pretty selective at times.

It helps to remember that I would not be alive today if I had not admitted my need and asked for help. My mind and body could not have survived this past year without a break from the hideous pain I was experiencing, both physically and emotionally.

Sometimes it helps to look back and see how far I've come so that I keep moving forward. It's not safe back there behind me!

———————————

Lord, help me let go of the past. Please give me the desire to keep moving.

And they were both naked, the man and his wife,
and were not ashamed.   —Gen. 2:25

At a support group one night, a woman shared that her husband had never seen her naked. They had three children, but she was so ashamed of her body that she hid it from him. I felt sad when I heard her story.

At the time I could not relate. Even though I was extremely overweight, I did not mind being naked in front of my husband. These days it's an entirely different story for me.

I'm well on my way to recovery, and I have shed most of my excess weight. So why am I ashamed of my body now? I think that I used to be in denial about how heavy I was. All that extra fat was serving as a layer of protection. At least if people didn't accept me, there was a reason.

The memories of sexual abuse that I'm working through have made me want to go under cover. I want my fat back! It made me feel very safe. I told myself that no one would want to get close to me if I was obese.

I am dealing with the issues that make me want to be fat again. I want to learn to deal with life without hiding, with or without my fat.

Father, help me face the things that make me feel ashamed. Teach me to trust you to protect me, so I don't have to put on an armor of fat.

> *And let us not grow weary while doing good, for in*
> *due season we shall reap if we do not lose heart.*
>
> —Gal. 6:9

I heard her read this verse time and time again in chapel. She hung on to it like a shipwrecked survivor hanging on to a life raft.

Twenty-three years old, she had been battling anorexia for ten years. She still clung to her childhood dream of having a happy family. Her disease allowed her parents to focus on something other than their own problems. Anorexia, the thing that was literally killing her, was resulting in something "good."

God used this woman to show me that all the "good" things I am working on may not be his plan for me. I involve myself in activities that seem beneficial, but at times I realize that they are not what's best for me.

I am learning to ask God to show me what he thinks is best!

Father, give me courage to continue doing what is your good; please give me wisdom to do what's best for me.

Teach me good judgment and knowledge,
For I believe Your commandments.
—Ps. 119:66

I have always worn my hair extremely short. I had not given much thought to my hair length until I entered treatment for my eating disorder. I realized that my short hair kept me from feeling feminine; it was a way to make me less attractive, and therefore less vulnerable to men. At the same time, my dad had always liked my hair short. So in order to please him I kept it that way.

My hair is down to my shoulders now. One reason I let it grow was to separate my identity from my parents. Also, I do not want to make myself look ugly just so I feel safe. But now I do not know if I am wearing my hair longer because I really want to, or because I know that's not how my dad likes my hair!

I want my decisions to be based on what is right. I no longer want to do things in reaction to others. With the knowledge I have been given I can make choices using my own good judgment. I want my plans to fall in line with what God wants for me. I can ask him for wisdom in making good choices.

Lord, teach me how to make wise decisions. Show me areas of my life that are not in line with your will.

> *The rich and the poor have this in common,*
> *The LORD is the maker of them all.*
>
> —Prov. 22:2

While I was in treatment I realized that an eating disorder serves as a real leveler. When it comes right down to it, we're all the same! The things that we do or have or attain in this life only count for a little while!

I was amazed to know that people I have always envied fall prey to the same pain I do. Rich people have had horrible things happen in their past. Women with gorgeous bodies still struggle with their self-image. Friends I know who look like they are "together" have turmoil in their lives as well.

Part of my delusion is that my life should be easy and that by doing right things I can avoid problems. What a set-up! Life is tough, and no one has got it made. Once I stop being surprised when bad things happen, I can take time to deal with trouble as it comes.

I can envy the woman with the perfect body at a distance, but I know that she has difficulties and stress, just as I do. We're all alike in that way.

Lord, teach me to accept life as it comes and to stop believing lies.

*And you who were once alienated and enemies
in your mind by wicked works, yet now He has
reconciled in the body of His flesh through death,
to present you holy, and blameless, and above
reproach in His sight.*   —Col. 1:21–22

A characteristic that I share with many of my friends
with eating disorders is alienation. Many of us have led
lonely, isolated lives.

At the height of my disease I isolated myself, both
emotionally and physically, from my friends and family. I turned down invitations to go places and remained distant in relationships.

I pulled away from people, and ultimately, from God;
I withdrew more and more into my loneliness. I believed that I deserved to be alone because I felt unworthy and unlovable. My feelings of self-hate stemmed
from my perfectionism. My failures in life loomed very
large; I tallied them up daily.

I realized that no one was expecting me to be perfect except myself. Most importantly, God did not expect me to be perfect; his love for me has never been
based on my performance. Now his grace allows me to
extend myself to others without being fearful of rejection.

I am lovable because Jesus loves me; I am worthy
because he is worthy! God sees me as holy and blameless through his Son.

Father, help me to accept myself as you do and help me start reaching out to others.

Judge not, that you be not judged.
—Matt. 7:1

Right now I believe everyone around me is judging me harshly. It hurts a lot when others judge me without knowing all the facts.

I must admit that I have also judged people. It is so easy to view things from my own vantage point and make snap judgments about what is best. I have been critical of friends who did not follow the guidelines that fit my agenda.

I am painfully aware of the fact that things are not always what they seem. After all, I am one who kept an eating disorder secret for thirteen years! I know that I acted out of extreme pain.

I am working hard to remind myself that others deal with pain in different ways. Not everyone chooses to abuse food to avoid life's pressure. I am learning to be more tolerant of differences in people. We're not all alike on the outside, but on the inside we're all pretty much the same.

Lord, teach me not to be judgmental. Remind me to make allowances for differences in others.

*Not that I have already attained, or am already
perfected; but I press on, that I may lay hold of that
for which Christ Jesus has also laid hold of me.*
—Phil. 3:12

I had high expectations for my recovery from eating
disorders! When I entered treatment at Remuda
Ranch, I thought I would leave there "fixed." I grew a
lot during the nine weeks I spent in treatment; my life
was literally transformed. I was no longer the same,
inside or out.

It has been a year now since the healing process began. One of the most important things I have learned is
that recovery is not a moment in time or an event; it is
a progressive journey. Many changes have taken place
in me, but there is still work to be done.

Some issues in my life are easier to deal with than
others. The obsession with food is less of a problem
now, but my thinking is still extremely negative. I tend
to be very hard on myself.

Abstinence is not my final frontier; there are many
areas of dysfunction left in me. I am continuing to chip
away at the old junk that was hiding underneath my
eating disorder.

I am grateful for the newness I sense in me, and I
rely on God to show me what needs to be worked on
next.

Father, stay close as I climb past this plateau.

> *Though I speak with the tongues of men and of*
> *angels, but have not love, I have become sounding*
> *brass or a clanging cymbal. And though I have the*
> *gift of prophecy, and understand all mysteries and*
> *all knowledge, and though I have all faith, so that*
> *I could move mountains, but have not love, I am*
> *nothing. And though I bestow all my goods to feed*
> *the poor, and though I give my body to be burned,*
> *but have not love, I am nothing.*
>
> —1 Cor. 13:1–3

God used this passage in a mighty way in my life! Sometimes my priorities are all out of whack. This is my version of these verses:

If I am able to abstain from bingeing and purging but have no love in my heart, what does it matter? If food is no longer controlling my life but I don't love my kids, who cares? Though I am no longer deceitful about money, if I am not honest with my husband, what difference does it make?

Although I am available to women in crisis, do I make special time for my relationship with God? If I am able to speak to groups on recovery from eating disorders but I'm not speaking to my brother, what does it mean? If I spend hours each day writing devotions but don't take time out for friends, I will be lonely and empty.

_____

Lord, teach me to value the things that really count!

I will meditate on the glorious splendor of Your majesty,
and on Your wondrous works. —Ps. 145:5

I enjoyed the scenery on a recent trip. It was an over-cast day in the mountains. The leaves were just beginning to change, and they dotted the dark green of the mountains with splashes of brilliant color. I felt revived as I took in the creation of God.

Not only did the picturesque setting thrill my heart, but I was also touched by my awareness of it! For so many years all I could think about was myself. I was absorbed in thoughts of my body and food to such an extent that I was oblivious to life around me.

After nine weeks in treatment, my view of life is beginning to get better. Life is not perfect; there is still pain to face, but it no longer consumes me. I feel like I am just coming to life. That is exciting, but it's also a little scary.

I am no longer numb to my feelings. I choose not to eat in reaction to the pain in my life. I am learning to cope with life without abusing my body.

When I hear my kids giggling in the family room or see a beautiful bird outside the window, I am glad that I lived long enough to really live!

Lord, I thank you for healing me so I can enjoy the beauty around me.

"These things I have spoken to you, that in Me you may have peace. In the world you will have tribulation; but be of good cheer, I have overcome the world."
—John 16:33

I am such a sucker! Somewhere along the way I was convinced that if I did my part, things would go smoothly. I always figured that if people had problems, they were doing something wrong. So my plan was to do the right thing and avoid trouble.

What a lie! This verse makes it plain that I will have tribulation. No matter what I do, I will have to face struggles and choose how to deal with them. There are many options for working through problems.

For many years I numbed myself with food. I restricted for a while, and then binged and purged. At times I compulsively overate and did not get rid of the excess calories. My eating disorder was an attempt to avoid dealing with life. Sadly, my problems were not solved by my abuse of food.

Now I choose not to dodge my problems behind mountains of food. I am working hard to face things head on. It is scary! I have had to learn new coping techniques. These new tools do not eliminate pain from my life any more than food did.

I am learning that there is peace to be found in God. I do not have to wait until life is problem-free to experience his peace!

Father, teach me to look to you in times of trouble.

*For he who serves Christ in these things is
acceptable to God and approved by men.*
—Rom. 14:18

No matter how well I do something, I am afraid that it will not be good enough. I want to be accepted and gain approval, but I pay dearly for it.

The exceptions I make for others do not apply to me. I don't mind if a friend is a few minutes late, but I do not allow myself that privilege. I do not think people are totally worthless if they say something inappropriate, but I feel devastated when my words are not perfect.

My mistakes seem overwhelming to me, and I have a hard time forgiving myself for being human. God has provided a means to deal with my imperfections. His Son died for my stupid remarks; he gave his life so that I can be late.

Because Christ Is in me, I am acceptable to God! I do not have to perform exceptionally well to gain his favor! I have already been approved. I used my eating disorder to numb myself from the guilt I felt over not being perfect. Now I have to learn to deal with my feelings in other ways.

I am learning to accept myself because God accepts me. I don't feel worthy of his love and approval, but I am acting as if I am. I hope the feelings will eventually follow.

Lord, help me to believe and feel your acceptance.

> *Yet in all these things we are more than conquerors*
> *through Him who loved us.* —Rom. 8:37

The statistics for recovering from eating disorders are bleak. When I visit support groups, it saddens me to see the despair among people who are struggling to free themselves from these vicious diseases.

I am more than a conqueror through Jesus Christ! This disease is not going to destroy me; I am on my way to becoming whole. I do not have the power to fight anorexia, bulimia, and compulsive overeating on my own, but with God's strength I will recover!

There are still days when I resist God's plan in my life. I want to do things my way, and I don't like admitting that I need his help to make it. Sometimes I forget that I had my way for thirteen years and it almost cost me my life.

Just beating this disease is not enough! I want to be more than a conqueror. I want to live a full, productive life, doing the things that God created me to do! I also want others to know that God can do more than just break the bonds of eating disorders.

I thank God for helping me conquer my disease! My abstinence has freed me to direct my energy toward things that go far beyond what I ever dreamed. Yes, I am a conqueror, but I am also much more!

Lord, thank you for allowing me to live long enough to conquer my eating disorder. Direct me now, please.

For God has not given us a spirit of fear, but of
power and of love and of a sound mind.
—2 Tim. 1:7

When I met her, her eyes held a kind of terror. I had the feeling that she was inside a body that didn't belong to her; she behaved like a cornered animal. At times it appeared that she might begin to trust others, but the spirit of fear was stronger than the desire to get well.

The pain from the past was manifested in her emaciated body. It was proof of fear's victory. As I prayed with her and told her of God's free gift of grace, I thought I saw a glimmer of hope in her eyes. I know she wanted to believe, but her fear was too great.

When I think of the pain in her eyes it breaks my heart! I am so thankful that God's love has cast the spirit of fear out of my life. He has brought power where there was none.

Father, thank you for removing my fears. Be with those who are stuck in pain and fear! Free them, Lord!

> *Commit your way to the LORD,*
> *Trust also in Him,*
> *And He shall bring it to pass.*
> —Ps. 37:5

Recovery Contract

I am committed to doing whatever it takes to preserve my recovery and my life. I have chosen to live, so I will do everything I can to stay alive. Even if the steps I must take seem uncomfortable or painful, I will follow through with my commitment.

I will guard against people and situations that threaten my ability to carry out my promise to live. Regardless of how I feel at the moment, I will do whatever it takes to stick to my plan of recovery. Doing these things may make me feel foolish, embarrassed, vulnerable, or irritated, but I will do them anyway because I am determined to recover.

I know that to give in to the pressure of others, or to be swayed by my fears could cost me my recovery and my life; therefore, I will go to any length to keep my focus on my recovery. I am willing to stay committed to my plan of recovery no matter how long it takes; I give myself the gift of time. I desire a solid foundation of health on which to build the rest of my life.

If I think that my commitment to life is weakening, I will do whatever it takes to strengthen my plan of recovery and preserve my life.

Father, strengthen my desire to live.

TERROR IN THE MARKET – *October 17*

She brings her food from afar. . . .
And provides food for her household.
—Prov. 31:14b, 15b

The grocery store holds a special kind of terror for me. Just walking through the aisles is enough to send shivers down my back! For many years the grocery store was my connection; it was the place I went to get my fix.

After being in treatment for nine weeks, I had to face my fears and start grocery shopping. At first I didn't go alone; I made sure I was with someone who understood how terrified I was. I hated to be in the store with all that food!

Eventually I was able to go shopping by myself, but I still had to talk myself through many of my fears. I had given the food so much power over me that it was hard to shop without feeling a huge emotional strain.

I try to make sure that I am not hungry when I shop. I also prepare a list beforehand so I am not tempted to buy unnecessary items. Talking to God really helps, too. He is willing to listen, and he doesn't think I'm silly for being fearful. I am learning to rely on his strength for things like grocery shopping.

Lord, thank you for being with me always, even in the store. Please free me from my fear of food.

> *If we confess our sins, He is faithful and just to*
> *forgive us our sins and to cleanse us from all*
> *unrighteousness.*
> —1 John 1:9

I accept the fact that God can forgive my sins. The problem is that I cannot forgive myself. I never forget one of my sins!

Shame is a big part of my identity. It started with my being sexually abused as a child. I felt as though I had done something wrong, that it was my fault it happened. As an adult I can logically understand that I did nothing to deserve sexual abuse. Now how do I get rid of the shame?

I am working to place the blame on the men who hurt me as a child. I remind myself that I am not responsible for their wrongdoing. Part of my healing is walking through the painful memories so that I may be free of the misplaced guilt and shame I feel.

Some of the shame is mine, because I have done things that were not acceptable in God's sight! Asking his forgiveness and accepting it helps me chip away at the mountain of shame. Eating never took away any of the shame; it only covered it up temporarily. Now I am practicing dealing with things head-on, so that I do not have to bury my shame under food.

Lord, forgive me and cleanse me from shame.

> *These things indeed have an appearance of wisdom
> in self-imposed religion, false humility, and neglect
> of the body, but are of no value against the
> indulgence of the flesh.*
> —Col. 2:23

During college I became obsessed with exercise. There were many areas of my life that were out of control, and I gained a sense of power by exercising compulsively.

I was able to focus on the physical pain in my body, rather than dealing with the pain and emptiness inside me. It gradually took more and more exercise to achieve the same false sense of well-being. The very control I desired escaped me as my life became consumed with my obsession.

My poor self-esteem was given a boost as I strengthened my body. I felt a sense of power, as though I was a better person than those who were not as "disciplined" as I was. Things looked great on the outside; I gained approval and acceptance from others who thought I had my life in order.

Although I had mastered my body, other areas of my life were sadly out of shape. I spent so much time in the gym that I was drained; there was no time in my life for my emotional and spiritual needs.

Today I am no longer controlled by exercise, and my life is more balanced! Growing stronger emotionally and spiritually takes away the drive to abuse my body.

Lord, I am grateful for the freedom from compulsivity.

*And by smooth words and flattering speech deceive
the hearts of the simple.* —Rom. 16:18

I just love hearing secrets; it makes me feel so special!
It flatters me when someone says, "Now this is just between you and me." With all my heart I long to know
that I am special and valuable.

There is a big cost in keeping secrets, though. I have
to keep track of which things can be shared with
others and which cannot. It's a lot of work to screen
everything that comes out of my mouth.

Some of the secrets that are shared with me put me
in quite a spot. When women share with me that they
are feeling suicidal, I must decide what to do with that
information. I must break their confidence in me or
risk feeling responsible if something bad happens.

Part of my eating disorder is keeping secrets. I hid
many things from people around me. For years my
husband never knew that I threw up everything I ate.
That was not a healthy secret to keep.

Honesty is one way to move toward wholeness. Although I enjoy being singled out for secrets, I am not
willing to pay the price for feeling special.

Father, help me to know that I am special to you.

*Look at the birds of the air, for they neither sow
nor reap nor gather into barns; yet your heavenly
Father feeds them. Are you not of more value
than they?*

—Matt. 6:26

For years I was so bitter and angry that it was difficult
to find anything good in life. I had such hatred in my
heart that I could not see how God was using situations
for my benefit.

I still have trouble accepting some events in my life. I
wonder how God could have allowed a little girl to be
abused time and time again. I have found the freedom
to tell God that I am angry for those things, and even
that I am angry at him for letting them take place.

Since my healing began my outlook on life has
changed! I see things happening that cause me to feel
loved. I am beginning to believe that God really cares
for me. I used to expect God to make life perfect and
pain-free, but I am now aware of his work in me because of the pain.

Little things, like a phone call from a friend, assure
me that I am loved. When I come across a fantastic
bargain, I like to look at it as a little gift from God.

The events that led up to my entering treatment for
my eating disorder were more than just a coincidence.
I know God allowed me to meet the right people so I
could begin the healing process.

Lord, thank you for taking care of me!

The LORD God is my strength;
He will make my feet like deer's feet,
And He will make me walk on my high hills.
　　　　　　　　　　　—Hab. 3:19

My recovery is like climbing Mount Everest. From the bottom I cannot see how far I must climb. I cannot even see the top of the mountain; it is obscured by the clouds.

At first I am excited about what lies ahead and the newness of the journey. As time passes each boulder begins to look like a mountain itself, and there are thousands of boulders for me to climb. Along the way it begins to rain, and I am afraid that the wind will blow me off the mountain. The weather grows colder, and I am unprepared for the inevitable blizzard.

I become discouraged, so I sit down and consider traveling back down the mountain. I would like to start over when the weather is better or when I'm in better shape. Do I really want to start over?

I notice the deer leaping from rock to rock as they make their way to the top of the mountain; they are so surefooted! At times they must seek shelter from the storms and stop to rest; still, they continue on toward their goal.

The Lord has given me what I need to be surefooted on my journey. It is not an easy path; there are many storms. He gives me shelter from the elements and the strength I need to walk in high places.

Lord, keep me going through the storms, always surefooted in you.

*And they heard the sound of the Lord God walking
in the garden in the cool of the day, and Adam and
his wife hid themselves from the presence of the
Lord God among the trees of the garden.*

—Gen. 3:8

Since entering treatment at Remuda Ranch for my
eating disorder, I have tried to be very honest. Many of
the shameful secrets I kept for years have been uncovered and no longer haunt me. I am much more free
to share myself in an open way and risk being vulnerable.

At times I resort to hiding again. I fear that if people
really knew what I was like, they would reject me. My
thoughts are so hideous at times, I think that I am the
only one in the world who has ever thought these
things.

Even in therapy I struggle to stay honest. After all, I
have to face that therapist again. What if I say something to make her think less of me? So I hide behind
safe, shallow topics and waste valuable time and
money in therapy.

God knew exactly where Adam and Eve were! He
even knew why they were hiding. Do I think I can fool
God about what's going on in my head? He knows my
fears, as well as the events in my past that caused me
to be fearful. No matter how hard I try, I cannot hide
from God.

---

*Lord, help me become so secure in your love that I no longer fear
being found out. Remind me that I do not have to hide from you.*

*Take My yoke upon you and learn from Me, for I
am gentle and lowly in heart, and you will find rest
for your souls. For My yoke is easy and My burden
is light.*
—Matt. 11:29–30

Long ago, oxen were yoked together to plow a farmer's fields. The farmer harnessed a young, inexperienced ox together with an older, experienced one. The older animal carried most of the burden for the younger one. The stronger ox could actually direct the work with the yoke.

I thought I had to recover on my own. I was afraid that it would be too much for me to handle, that it would be too hard. But I discovered that Jesus was offering to carry the heaviest part of my burden for me. Jesus wants me to be yoked with him; he wants to teach me and guide me.

Christ has never grabbed the load out of my grasp. My heavenly Father has taken whatever part of the load I trusted him with, and waited patiently for me to give him more.

At first I wanted to be in control of the harness, but it was too heavy and I fell beneath the weight of it. I learned that I had to let go and allow Jesus to lead the way and direct the work. I am finding rest for my soul yoked to my gentle Savior.

Dearest Jesus, give me the courage to let you carry me through my recovery.

Be merciful to me, O God, be merciful to me!
For my soul trusts in You;
And in the shadow of Your wings I will make my refuge,
Until these calamities have passed by.   —Ps. 57:1

My daughter is battling bulimia, a disease which is rooted in her childhood. A neighborhood boy molested her when she was only four. She didn't have the emotional skills to deal with that pain. Instead she swept away the memory of it, like dust under some thick rug.

Every mother's nightmare has come true in my life! My mistakes in parenting have contributed greatly to my child's pain. I'd like to go to bed, wake up in the morning, and discover this whole miserable situation is only a bad dream.

I am heartsick; there is nothing I can do to change the events which have caused my daughter such pain. My only hope is to seek refuge in God until this destruction passes.

_____

Lord, you are a perfect Father. Help me give my daughter what she needs from me today. I trust you to make up for my inadequacy.

> *Do not lie to one another, since you have put off*
> *the old man with his deeds.*   —Col. 3:9

Lately I have perfected a new way of lying. I don't say things that are untrue; I just don't say anything at all. I have convinced myself that my thoughts and feelings are worthless, so I do not say what I need to say.

When I keep silent I feel victimized again. I feel angry and resentful because I compromise my standards. Still, my self-esteem is so low that I reason that others must know what is best.

Recently I was asked to do something that went against my morals. Instead of assertively stating my views, I ignored my conscience and went along with the request. I felt a lot of guilt. There were several times during the process when I could have voiced my objections, but I resisted.

It seemed easier at the time to give in to what was being asked. I also did not want to risk being rejected. I was afraid that if I shared my opinion, others would think I was silly or ignorant. So I lied by not speaking at all. In the end I had to correct my lies. It would have been much simpler to tell the truth in the first place.

Lord, teach me to be truthful at any cost.

But you are a chosen generation, a royal priesthood, a holy nation, His own special people, that you may proclaim the praises of Him who called you out of darkness into His marvelous light.
—1 Peter 2:9

I get so excited when I think about the changes that have taken place in my life in the last year! It is hard to believe that I am the same person who was so desperate and suicidal just one year ago.

After thirteen years of struggling with eating disorders I finally hit bottom, and it was not a pleasant experience. That's what it took for me to get well, though, so I am thankful that I lived to reach that point.

When I entered treatment at Remuda Ranch I was frightened and angry. I had lived much of my life in fear, so I had experienced little of what the world had to offer. I had used food to numb myself for so long that I was not equipped to cope with life. The tools I received in treatment have helped prepare me to live.

In the last year I have come to life! In the past I never allowed myself to take risks because I was too fearful of failure. Now I am involved in things that seem way beyond me! I have found that it is all right to risk; making a mistake does not mean I am a failure! God has brought me out of the pain and darkness of my eating disorder. It feels a lot different in the light, but I love it. I want to live!

_____

Father, I thank you for bringing me out of the dark.

> *As far as the east is from the west,*
> *So far has He removed our transgressions from us.*
> —Ps. 103:12

I am so grateful that God does not store up my sins in a big pile like I do. God doesn't even keep a log of all the ugly things I've done; he has removed my sins from me! Unfortunately, being forgiven does not eliminate the natural consequences of my sins.

I wish that making right choices today would erase all the negative results of the poor choices I made yesterday. Unfortunately it does not work that way! My sins have been paid for, but I still have to deal with the results here on earth.

For instance, when I admitted that I had an eating disorder, I thought my family would be thrilled that I was being honest and seeking help. Instead, they were angry and hurt that I had deceived them for years.

I have not binged or purged for nine months now, but my body is still paying for the years of abuse.

Since I left treatment, I have not spent money compulsively or stolen from the household budget. My husband is still reluctant to leave financial decisions up to me; I have to work to regain his trust.

Today I want to make wise choices. Doing what's right now will lessen the consequences later.

Lord, help me learn from my mistakes, please!

Go, eat your bread with joy,
And drink your wine with a merry heart;
For God has already accepted your works.
—Eccl. 9:7

As I move ahead in recovery, food is slowly losing its power over me. Some days I am not controlled by thoughts of food. I am not always obsessed with my body.

I have learned that I am acceptable to God. Right now, this very moment, with all my imperfections, God loves me. His love is not contingent upon my losing or gaining weight. He will not love me more when I firm up those flabby spots.

At times I actually enjoy eating! It is so freeing to eat without being consumed by fear. Visiting with friends over lunch is fun; no one else is looking at my plate to estimate the total calories.

I love to entertain guests in my home; it brings me joy to know that my food is good. But my identity is no longer based on my culinary ability. I used to seek approval with my cooking, and I felt like a failure if every dish was not perfect.

God has accepted me! That makes it easier to deal with burned cookies and meals that don't look like the picture in the cookbook.

Father, help me learn to enjoy eating food.

October 30 – ALL BY MYSELF

*Again, if two lie down together, they will keep warm;
But how can one be warm alone?*
—Eccl. 4:11

I was a father who had it "all together," a businessman who was busy building an empire. I allowed people to need me, but I presented myself as needing no one. I believed I could accomplish anything I set my hand to, without help from others.

This "strength" that I had gathered over the years was my way of dealing with life. I had no idea how destructive it was to the ones I loved.

Suddenly my life was out of control! My daughter had been diagnosed with "anorexia nervosa"; she was purposely starving herself. This did not fit in my plan at all. I did not know how to handle this problem on my own.

God used my daughter's eating disorder to show me that I had needs—plenty of them! I needed the advice of doctors and other people who had dealt with this disease. Most of all, I needed wisdom from God to know how to deal with my daughter.

My recovery from being self-reliant has been a long, hard process. I find myself taking two steps forward, and then one step back, but I am committed to this journey. I have learned that I do need people in my life, and with God's guidance, I am allowing myself to show people I have needs.

————————

Lord, I can't do this alone; I need you!

Then Jesus said to him, "Away with you, Satan! For it is written, 'You shall worship the LORD your God, and Him only you shall serve.'" —Matt. 4:10

I know several women who have been horribly brutalized in ritualistic ceremonies related to Halloween. Their lives have been crippled by the anguish of the awful memories that live within them. Many people have failed to support them, saying, "That doesn't really happen, at least not in my town. Besides, Halloween is harmless."

I do not want to be naive about what is really happening in my world. It's easy to want to bury my head in the sand and deny the pain my friends are facing, but that does not make it any less real.

This has caused me to take a close look at the activities I choose. I want my life to honor God, and I do not want to pay tribute to any of the gods of this world.

My eating disorder started out in a harmless way; I thought it was a great way to take off my weight. I have since learned that my fear of becoming fat covered some deep-seated problems in me.

Lord, I want to serve you with my life.

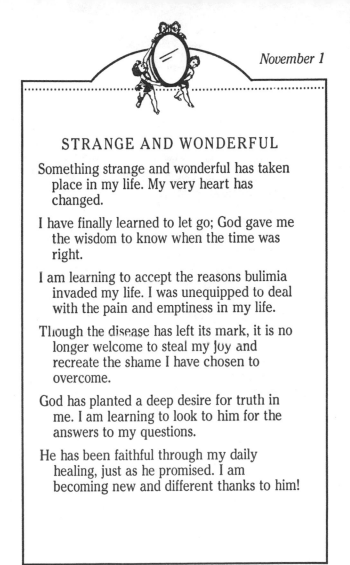

STRANGE AND WONDERFUL

Something strange and wonderful has taken place in my life. My very heart has changed.

I have finally learned to let go; God gave me the wisdom to know when the time was right.

I am learning to accept the reasons bulimia invaded my life. I was unequipped to deal with the pain and emptiness in my life.

Though the disease has left its mark, it is no longer welcome to steal my joy and recreate the shame I have chosen to overcome.

God has planted a deep desire for truth in me. I am learning to look to him for the answers to my questions.

He has been faithful through my daily healing, just as he promised. I am becoming new and different thanks to him!

And those who know Your name will put their trust in You;
For You, LORD, have not forsaken those who seek You.
—Ps. 9:10

In the midst of my eating disorder, I often doubted God's presence in my life. I made many promises not to purge anymore, but I continued to do it. I believed that God was unable to love me because I could not keep my promise to him.

Through all my doubts, I held on to the hope that God had not rejected me. Without that slim hope, I would have had no reason to go on living. I found strength in the book of Psalms in the Bible. I read that David experienced many of the same feelings I did. I found hope in the promises of God's Word.

God has promised not to forsake those who seek him. I don't have to do everything right or be perfect for God to be available to me. The only thing I have to do is seek him.

I believe he understands my times of doubt and fear. He stands ready to spread his wings of love over me and draw me to him.

Father, thank you for your promise never to forsake me.

*Stand fast therefore in the liberty by which Christ
has made us free, and do not be entangled again
with a yoke of bondage.* —Gal. 5:1

Father, I am no longer controlled by my obsession
with food; and for that I am grateful. I am now able to
deal with life without turning to food to hide. Thank
you, Lord, for freeing me from the external behaviors
of my eating disorder.

I want to be released from the bondage of perfectionism! My critical attitude toward myself and others
is devastating. The unhealthy thought processes of a
lifetime are hard to beat, but I know there is hope in
you.

I hate the part of me that is never satisfied; I see the
pain in my children's eyes when I expect too much
from them. I have felt that pain, Lord. I know what it is
to be expected to do more than is humanly possible. I
don't want to wound my children in this way.

Lord, I am grateful for the work you are doing in my
life! I see changes in many areas, and that is encouraging to me. Please continue to make me new.

Father, I admit to you that I am powerless to heal
myself from perfectionism on my own. I know you are
able to do what needs to be done. Please make my
heart willing to be changed. I need you, Father. Help
me!

Dear Lord,

It's almost time for the holidays, and that really scares me. This is my first holiday season without choosing the option of bingeing and purging. Thank you for giving me the desire to get help and get well so I really do have some options.

When I saw all the Christmas stuff in the stores I panicked! I don't feel ready; I have been busy working on my recovery, and a whole year slipped by me. The idea of a year being gone is really sobering, Lord. I'm not sure this is where I wanted to be one year out of treatment.

Facing piles of food and relatives at the same time is pretty overwhelming. Please remind me of my options. I do not have to do anything just because it's "what we've always done." Give me the strength to start new traditions.

Lord, I am proud of the progress I've made in my recovery in this last year. I don't want to jeopardize it for the sake of an extra helping of stuffing. Please remind me to rely on you for the strength to make wise choices about food.

I thank you for being concerned about the things that are important to me. Help me to be concerned with what is important to you. I want to remember what the holiday season is all about. Amen.

Jesus answered and said to him, "If anyone loves Me, he will keep My word; and My Father will love him, and We will come to him and make Our home with him. . . ."

And yet I am not alone, because the Father is with Me.
                                        —John 14:23; 16:32

I have been adopted into God's family by accepting Jesus as my Savior. I have acknowledged that I need God in my life. The result is that God now makes his home in me!

For years I thought, "God couldn't love me, not with all the secrets in my past!" My shame and guilt kept me from accepting what God had to offer me. It was hard to believe that he saw what was inside me and loved me anyway.

At first I did not believe it could be true, but with a tiny seed of faith, I asked God to show himself to me. I really hated being alone, and I liked the idea of having God with me at all times. I wanted to believe that he could free me from all my shame.

Today I am grateful that I was able to believe God's Word, if only with a tiny part of my heart. God does reside within me, and I never have to be alone again.

Thank you, Lord, for being with me and in me.

And not only that, but we also glory in tribulations,
knowing that tribulation produces perseverance;
and perseverance, character; and character, hope.
Now hope does not disappoint, because the love of
God has been poured out in our hearts by the Holy
Spirit who was given to us. —Rom. 5:3–5

I still suffer from the fear of rejection, but now I have new choices to make. Prior to treatment for my eating disorder, and before I knew what it was to have hope in God, my fears caused me to build walls of self-protection. I was so absorbed with myself that I sabotaged every relationship I had.

At that time I could not imagine being joyful about suffering. Instead, I dug an emotional pit and allowed myself to sink into hopelessness and despair. I used food to numb me from the pain in my life.

Looking back, I see how God used my suffering to develop the hope I have today. That hope, together with my faith in God, allows me to make new choices. Rather than allowing myself to get caught in the downward spiral of fear, I choose to live in the knowledge of God's love and acceptance.

Accepting the depth of God's love for me allows me to take chances; I can risk being rejected by others because I know God's love for me is unconditional.

Father, I accept and rejoice in my suffering. I see how you have used it to mold my character.

Father,

It's the time of the year when food is a big focus. There seems to be food everywhere I look! People act like it doesn't bother them, but I feel panicky.

My nutritionist says I am beginning to eat "normally and spontaneously." That sounds terrifying to me! I have never felt normal about anything, especially not my eating. Why am I afraid to get well?

This "normal" eating does not feel safe; I'm afraid that I'm going to turn into a blimp. I have started to take risks with my food. Sometimes I eat food just because I want to, not because it's necessary. I am learning to enjoy food.

That worries me—I'm afraid that I will start to enjoy it too much. I feel guilty for eating food that is not on my food plan. I think, "Will people judge me for eating something when I look like I do?" It's really hard to get away from my preoccupation with what others think.

Lord, I don't see myself the way others do. It is hard to get a clear picture of the way my body looks. I don't believe what people say about my weight, but I know that my thinking is distorted. Please help me see myself accurately.

I want to be relaxed and comfortable during the holidays. So please take away all my fears. I am choosing to allow myself to eat, but I do not want to overdo it. Please give me wisdom and discernment when I make choices about eating. Amen.

Like an earring of gold and an ornament of fine gold
Is a wise rebuker to an obedient ear. —Prov. 25:12

It is hard to accept criticism, even when it's constructive! It is painful to find out that others are aware of my defects of character.

A person I trust pointed out some areas in my life that need attention. She was right, of course; she knows me well. But I am now struggling to put the advice in perspective.

Part of me is so weak and frail that I want to figure out what's wrong with my friend. I wonder why she would hurt me like this. I want to find a way to discount her words; I don't want to be responsible for this information.

My natural tendency is to reach for food to comfort me. "Chocolate might help," I think. My insides are aching and I want to stop the pain. Past experience tells me that the chocolate is not the answer. It will taste good going down, but then I will have to deal with the feelings of guilt. I'll feel fat and ugly. It's just not worth it!

I am learning to work through the pain of life in new ways! I am thankful for friends who care enough about me to say what I need to hear.

Lord, thank you for speaking through those around me. Make me willing to listen.

Cease listening to instruction, my son,
And you will stray from the words of knowledge.
—Prov. 19:27

At this point, I feel like I've had enough! After nine weeks of inpatient treatment for my eating disorder and months of support groups and therapy, I want a break! I do not want to hear one more thing about how unhealthy I still am.

I feel like giving up; I wonder if I will ever be whole. But I will not give in to my negative thoughts. I have come too far to let all this work go to waste. I will not stop doing the things that have saved my life.

My support groups and therapy are plain old hard work, and I will continue to make the effort. I choose to listen to what others have to say; it gives me insight into my own issues.

I am aware that to discontinue my plan of recovery would surely mean disaster! This path to wellness is not easy, but it is worth it to get well. I know there are changes taking place in me, and that makes me willing to persevere.

Father, you know how tired I feel. Please give me the strength to endure. Make me willing to listen to advice from those whom you have placed in my life.

> *A word fitly spoken is like apples of gold*
> *In settings of silver.*   —Prov. 25:11

I have felt discouraged many times during my recovery. This is a struggle like none I have ever faced, and it is too big for me to face alone.

God has used the encouragement of others to keep me going. He has provided me with a few people who are loving and accepting of me and my recovery. Hearing words from these trusted few has made such a difference in my healing.

It seems like whenever I am ready to quit, someone is there to give me a boost. My support groups have been instrumental in providing regular, gentle feedback when I need it.

Still, sometimes I feel like I am all alone! People are not always available to me, but in those moments I hear God speaking words of love. In a still, small voice he reminds me that I am his child. I am acceptable to him, and he loves me no matter what! Those words are precious to me.

Father, thank you for touching my heart with words from you and others.

The LORD is my light and my salvation;
Whom shall I fear?
The LORD is the strength of my life;
Of whom shall I be afraid?

—Ps. 27:1

Many people are surprised when I tell them that I am basically a very shy person. It is hard for me to meet new people and go into unfamiliar situations, but I am more confident than I used to be.

For years I let my eating disorder shield me from dealing with my fears. I was bound up in timidity; I hated to be a bother to anyone, so I rarely expressed my needs. Assuming that people would not like me, I was reluctant to pursue new relationships. As time went on, I became more and more fearful of taking risks.

Since I began my recovery, I have become less timid. I am still shy, but now I am able to enter new situations instead of running from them. Meeting new people is still a fear, but I know I can face the challenges of life! The Spirit of God lives in me, and I am learning to rely on his strength when I am afraid.

Lord, I thank you for the courage to overcome my fears.

> *I will praise You, O LORD, with my whole heart;*
> *I will tell of all Your marvelous works.*
> *I will be glad and rejoice in You;*
> *I will sing praise to Your name, O Most High.*
> —Ps. 9:1–2

For years, I was ruled by my emotions. Instead of living by the motto, "If it feels good, do it," my slogan was, "If it doesn't feel good, don't do it!"

Many mornings I didn't feel like getting out of bed because my depression was so great. I canceled many dates with friends because I didn't feel up to getting ready. I prayed only when I felt close to God.

In this psalm David does not say, "I praise you because I feel like doing it." There were times when he felt discouraged, but David did what he knew God wanted him to do. He trusted God to bless his effort.

Recovery, like life, is sometimes just putting one foot in front of the other, regardless of feelings. There are still mornings when I don't feel like getting out of bed; doing what I need to do makes it easier to push through my feelings the next time I feel blue. I have found that saying "I will" means I can!

Lord, give me the strength to act on what I know, rather than how I feel.

That I may proclaim with the voice of thanksgiving,
And tell of all Your wondrous works.

—Ps. 26:7

I am learning to be thankful! For years I was so bitter and angry and full of shame that I couldn't be thankful for anything. Since I began my recovery from eating disorders, my heart is full of thanks.

Much of the guilt and shame that had colored my thinking is gone. I was able to separate the guilt over things I had done from the misplaced guilt I felt for others' wrongdoing. I still tend to feel guilty for things that are not my responsibility, but I am able to talk myself out of that most of the time.

I am thankful today for my new-found freedom from compulsion with food. With food in its proper place I am able to function more normally! Life is still painful at times, but I know that abusing my body with food does not make the pain stop.

I look forward to celebrating Thanksgiving with a grateful heart. I am starting some new holiday traditions this year; I do not have to resort to old habits when it comes to food. I have new options, and I'm thankful for that! I want to focus on things I am thankful for and to enjoy the food I eat without feeling guilty.

Lord, I thank you for this new grateful feeling in my heart.

> *For he will not dwell unduly on the days of his life,*
> *because God keeps him busy with the joy of his*
> *heart.*
> —Eccl. 5:20

I have a hard time letting go of the little stuff in life. My memory never misses anything! The most insignificant detail can grow to alarming proportions in my mind! I obsess over meaningless comments from people. This practice makes for some pretty scary thoughts!

For the first time in my life, I have the ability to choose; I have options that were never before available to me. The trouble is, I don't know what I want to do. What will bring joy to my life? Having the option is great, but now what?

I am learning to give my obsessive thoughts to God. After all, staying stuck in my head keeps me from dealing with the issues at hand. Analyzing every remark made by others effectively paralyzes me from being productive.

I choose to invest some effort into finding out what I can do with my life. Now that I am not controlled by thoughts of food all day long, I have something to offer!

Father, please show me what I can do with my life. I want to find joy in the moment, rather than dwelling on senseless thoughts.

So when they were filled, He said to His disciples,
"Gather up the fragments that remain, so that
nothing is lost."
—John 6:12

At times I believe that my life was shattered into thousands of tiny pieces. The pain of the past, along with my current battle with an eating disorder, has left me wondering if I am salvageable. I am afraid that the little bits of my life are not worth saving.

God has begun to give me hope that he can use the bits and pieces of my life to recreate something worthwhile. I sense him tenderly gathering up the shredded pieces of my heart and holding them close.

I gain inspiration by viewing the beautiful art of stained glass. It is fashioned from tiny fragments of colored glass. The end result is not an accident, but an intricately designed piece of art work. In the same way, my Lord is working with the broken pieces of my life to create a work of art. He is using my body, which has been torn apart by an eating disorder, and the pain of my past to fashion a creation of beauty.

Father, please be tender with the pieces of my heart.

I said, "I will confess my transgressions to the LORD,"
And You forgave the iniquity of my sin. —Ps. 32:5

I have come to believe that self-abuse is sin. I sin when I refuse to give my body enough calories to flourish. My body was created to house God's Holy Spirit.

I do not honor God when I stand over the toilet and rid myself of food. If I choose to neglect my family while I spend hours exercising, I am not doing the job God gave me.

While I kept silent about my eating disorder I was engulfed in shame. Looking a friend in the eye was more than I could bear. I always feared that people would know my secret. I was afraid they would see how unlovable I was if they knew what I was really like. I hid myself from others.

When I allowed my sins to be exposed to the light of Christ, I found acceptance and forgiveness; I no longer had to hide myself. When I confessed, God forgave me! I am now able to experience his love for me.

Lord, I am grateful that your love and forgiveness never run dry.

*And he walked in all the sins of his father, which
he had done before him; his heart was not loyal to
the LORD his God, as was the heart of his father
David.*
                                        —1 Kings 15:3

God is really doing a work in my heart! It is a painful
process, but I am beginning to see that I am not totally
committed to God. As horrible as that may seem, it
helps me to know it so I can make changes in my loyalty.

I blindly accepted my parents' faith in God as my
own, and I never had to make my own connection with
him. I am now sifting through what my parents believed and making my own decisions about how it applies to my life with God.

This is just another step in my healing. God has used
my eating disorder to start a process of change in me. I
thought that the eating disorder was my only problem,
but underneath my obsession with food lay many
other areas of need.

Taking a close look at my spirituality is very scary to
me, but I am willing to work out my own relationship
with God. I want my loyalty to be to God and his Son
Jesus, not to my parents' religious beliefs.

*Father, I am fearful of this journey. Thank you for showing me where
my loyalty has been and where it needs to be.*

November 18 – GIVE ME UNDERSTANDING

> *So Jesus said, "Are you also still without understanding?"*
>
> —Matt. 15:16

Dear Lord,

I just don't get it! I have grown up in church, and I can recite numerous verses from the Bible. I have spent hours listening to teaching from your Word. So why is my life still a wreck?

I understand the principles in my head, but it is hard to make them work in my life. I know what I have to do, but I have trouble making myself do it.

The biggest problem I see is that I am still trying to do things in my own strength, and I do not trust you to take care of me. Lord, it hurts me to even admit those things. I feel like a failure.

I see the work you have done in my life in the area of my eating disorder. I'm thankful for that, Father, but I guess I want more! I want my life to count for something, and I don't even know what I want to do.

Thank you, Lord, for making me aware of new options; now could you give some direction, please? I am so afraid! I do not know what to do. I need to know what you want for me.

I do not know how to stop trying and doing and start being. I need help, Lord. Help me stop moving long enough to listen to your directions. Please talk above all the other voices I hear. I need to know that you are here! Amen.

*Each one's work will become clear; for the Day will
declare it, because it will be revealed by fire; and
the fire will test each one's work, of what sort it is.*
— 1 Cor. 3:13

During the course of my recovery, several people
have commented that I was doing good work. They
were referring to the fact that I was dealing with issues
in an honest manner and was willing to face things,
even when it was painful.

Hearing others talk about my progress is still uncomfortable for me. I have a hard time accepting the
fact that I am doing something well. It was also strange
to hear that "good work" was what I was doing. My
idea of good work was always avoiding pain at all cost!
My concept of what's good did not include crying, hurting, or even thinking about painful subjects.

I realize now that I spent my life trying not to face
issues that were unpleasant. I stuffed myself with food
to keep my feelings in check, and relieved myself of
anger and guilt in the toilet when I could no longer
stand it.

Now there are changes taking place in my life! The
factors that led to my disease are painful to face, but
God has given me the courage to continue doing "good
work."

*Lord, thank you for helping me do good work. I ask that you continue
to be with me through the process.*

> *Do not be unequally yoked together with*
> *unbelievers. For what fellowship has righteousness*
> *with lawlessness? And what communion has light*
> *with darkness?*
> —2 Cor. 6:14

I was the life of the party, and could always be counted on to bake extravagant, irresistible dishes for every get-together. I found much of my value in pleasing others; cooking and eating were a big part of my life.

Since I began my recovery from anorexia, bulimia, and compulsive overeating, my tactics have had to change. I am no longer willing to have food as the central focus of every activity. I have chosen to involve myself with people who do not feed my weaknesses.

This has meant I've had to make some changes in friendships. Many of the people who used to be my "binge buddies" are no longer interested in me since I am not practicing compulsive behaviors.

As painful as this has been, I am making new friends. God has brought people into my life who are supportive of the changes I am making. Since they did not know me before, they have no expectations of receiving lavish food gifts.

When I first let go of my obsession with food there was a big void in my life, but now I am learning to let God fill me up with things that are more significant than food.

Lord, it really hurts to lose friendships, even the unhealthy ones. Please mend my heart.

But he who endures to the end shall be saved.
—Matt. 24:13

I find myself obsessing about the time it's taking me to get well. I want to know how long it will be before I am "whole." I get so caught up in the future that it's hard to focus on the business at hand.

I have a standing joke with a friend of mine. When I think I cannot take another step on my path of recovery, I ask her, "How many more days?" She always tells me I just have to hang on for twenty-nine more days! Then when I get panicked again, she says, "Just another twenty-nine more days to go!"

Big family dinners end up being like that, too. Whenever there are lots of people around, it seems to take forever to get the food on the table. When serving time keeps being delayed I find it hard to wait. It's hard to endure when I'm hungry.

At any rate, I am enduring the process of recovery from my eating disorder! I am being saved from the disease that threatened my life for thirteen years. Although it is painful, I choose to keep taking one baby step at a time. No matter how many days it takes, I am committed to becoming all that God intended!

Lord, give me the strength and courage to endure!

> *Therefore do not worry about tomorrow, for*
> *tomorrow will worry about its own things.*
> *Sufficient for the day is its own trouble.*
>
> —Matt. 6:34

I can allow many obsessive thoughts to control my mind. I often worry about what I will do with my life. I wonder how my children will escape the dysfunction they have witnessed in me. I don't know what to do with myself, now that I am free from my eating disorder.

Today is more than enough for me! Each new day has plenty of challenges to face, without concerning myself with what is yet to come. Projecting far into the future keeps me from living right now. I know that at times the pain of the present is hard to stand, but escaping into worries of the future does not eliminate the pain. It only prolongs the inevitable.

I am learning to take things as they come. Of course, there is a risk of going to the other extreme with my thoughts. I would love to completely ignore the future, and not make responsible choices. The balance is hard to find.

Today I have tasks to complete. I choose to do my best to accomplish what is mine to do this day. I will follow my food plan, reach out for help when I need it, and apply myself to living this day as I believe God wants me to!

_____

Father, help me learn to put yesterday, today, and tomorrow into proper perspective.

He who loves father or mother more than Me is not worthy of Me. And he who loves son or daughter more than Me is not worthy of Me.

—Matt. 10:37

Much of my life has been spent trying to protect those around me. I kept all kinds of secrets in order to save those I loved from pain. Somehow I had the idea that it was my responsibility to make everyone happy. Ultimately, the cost of trying to fulfill that role was my health.

In order to appease others I sacrificed myself, my truth, and my body. I punished my body with an eating disorder because I felt guilt over my inability to meet everyone's expectations. My outlet from the pressure of life was food. It became my only comfort when all around me were lies and craziness.

I realize now that I was more fearful of letting my parents down than I was of disappointing God. I was afraid to let my children know that I had an eating disorder, but God knew all along.

My relationships with others were based on lies and deception. They loved the person that I pretended to be. God saw through all the masks, and he loved me anyway!

I am learning to let go of all that I once held dear. God is now most important to me.

Lord, remind me when you are not first in my heart.

*And the L ORD, the God of their fathers, sent word
to them again and again by His messengers,
because He had compassion on His people and on
His dwelling place; but they continually mocked the
messengers of God, despised His words, and scoffed
at His prophets, until the wrath of the L ORD arose
against His people, until there was no remedy.*
—2 Chron. 36:15–16 NAS

I chose to ignore many messengers along the way.
Friends questioned me about my varying weight, but I
always managed to come up with an excuse. Dentists
remarked about the condition of my teeth, and I kept
silent about my eating disorder.

I recall watching talk shows on television on the
topic of anorexia and bulimia. I was in such a state of
denial that I could not make the connection between
me and those diseases. It was as though I had lied to
people for so long that I began to believe the lies myself!

At one point my mother asked me, "How close were
you to having an eating disorder?" I said, "I was very
close." Not only was I close, I had been practicing one
for thirteen years!

I am so grateful to God for saving me before the
messengers quit coming. It breaks my heart to see
others who are not receptive to the message of health.

*Lord, thank you for sending messengers to save me! Please use my
recovery as a message to others who have not yet begun to get well.*

And even now the ax is laid to the root of the trees.
Therefore every tree which does not bear good fruit
is cut down and thrown into the fire.

—Matt. 3:10

I am grateful for many months of abstinence from disordered eating. I thank God for the work he has done in my life in that area. My outward behaviors have changed greatly, but my thoughts and feelings are much the same as they were when I was practicing my disease.

Once I stopped bingeing and purging my way through life, I had to take a look at what was underneath my obsession with food. I had avoided dealing with the pain; it was much easier to focus on external behaviors. As I continue in therapy, more and more issues come to the surface. It is such hard work!

God is gently pushing me to get at the roots of my eating disorder. I have found that changing my thought patterns comes from allowing God to cut out the unhealthy roots in my life.

I imagined that once I "got my eating under control" everything else would simply fall into place. That has not been the case. Instead, God has made me aware of the origin of my feelings of self-hatred and unworthiness. I have asked him to remove those things from my life. He is now pulling them out by the roots; it's a painful, but necessary process.

Lord, thank you for showing me the roots of my pain; hold me close as you weed out that junk!

> *"Have I not commanded you? Be strong and of good courage; do not be afraid, nor be dismayed, for the LORD your God is with you wherever you go."*
> —Josh. 1:9

Two weeks after I left treatment for my eating disorder, I was invited to a Super Bowl party. In typical bulimic fashion, I told myself, "You should be able to handle this; go ahead!" It was one of many close calls that I had early in my recovery.

A huge crowd was there and the table was loaded with food. As the game progressed, I nibbled and snacked on the assortment of goodies. All at once, my emotions took control! I felt out of control and feared that I had eaten too much.

I found a quiet spot and made a phone call for support. I was in tears as I told my friend where I was and what I had eaten. As I shared, she calculated how much I had consumed. When we talked about my "binge," I realized that I had not eaten more than I should have. It had simply felt overwhelming because it had not been a regular meal, eaten all at once.

After that I tried to prepare myself for new situations with food by getting information ahead of time; that way I felt more comfortable. It is not always possible to know the menu in advance, but I am learning to ask God for wisdom in my food choices. He is with me wherever I go, even to Super Bowl parties and church potlucks.

Father, remind me that you are near when I feel overwhelmed about food.

Set your mind on things above, not on things on the earth.
—Col. 3:2

I can't seem to stop obsessing about food. I am consumed by my fear of food and my drive to be thin. I spend countless hours each day considering what to put in my mouth. Much of my life is wasted calculating calories and protecting my secret, an eating disorder. There is not much time left to invest in things that really matter.

My social life is stifled by anorexia. I feel the need to control my eating, and it is difficult to do that when others are present. That makes being alone seem more inviting.

It is such a struggle to be productive at work while I am controlled by food. I find my mind wandering when I should be concentrating on other things. My disease robs me of the ability to give my full attention to my work.

At times, I believe I have replaced God with anorexia. I worship the disease that is slowly drawing life out of me. I give praise to thinness and starvation, when God is really the one worthy of my adoration.

God, please free me from this bondage of obsessive thoughts and actions

> *Therefore the people contended with Moses, and said, "Give us water, that we may drink." So Moses said to them, "Why do you contend with me? Why do you tempt the LORD?"*
>
> —Ex. 17:2

At times my children try my love; they seem to want to test me. It is as though they are saying, "Will Mom still love me, no matter how awful I act?" It is hard to put up with them then.

I am sure my heavenly Father knows that I test him at times. I try to see if he will always love me like he has promised. I am much like my children, and I wonder if his love and patience will last.

Often I spend my days whining and moaning and feeling sorry for myself. At times I let anger and self-centeredness rule my life. It is hard to believe God loves me even though I have an eating disorder.

I not only walk, but run, down the wrong path some days. Like a little child, I take off and won't stop for anything! I remember my children running away from me in the grocery store when they were little; it was as if they wanted to see how far they could push me.

I love my children! Sometimes their actions annoy me, but they are still my kids. When I think of my own limited ability to love, I am aware that God loves more than any human is capable of doing. He does withstand the test! His love is indescribable and infinite.

Father, I want to stop testing you and start trusting.

*For you were bought at a price; therefore glorify
God in your body and in your spirit, which are
God's.*
—1 Cor. 6:20

I have always loved to shop! I could spend hours in the
mall looking in the stores. When I saw an outfit I liked
especially well I told my mother, "I would do anything
for that." Often she would make a deal with me. She
would come up with a list of chores for me to do in
order to earn the desired item.

After I was presented with the cost, it was up to me
to decide if I was willing to work for what I wanted.
Many times I decided that the price was too high, and I
was not willing to earn the clothes. I thought, "Doing
dishes once might be all right, but I won't do them for a
whole week. That outfit isn't worth it!"

Recovery has worked much the same way for me.
There is a high cost to pay for getting well, and
at times I have felt unwilling to make the effort. Part of
the price is giving up habits that have become familiar
to me. I also have to follow my plan of recovery in
order to get healthy. That includes the cost of going to
groups and therapy when I'd rather do other things.

I have made the choice to "go the distance"! I am
willing to pay the price, no matter what it is, to be free
of my eating disorder. I am reminded that Christ paid
the price so that I might live. His example gives me the
strength to do whatever I have to do.

Lord, make my heart willing to pay the price.

> *And he arose and came to his father. But when he*
> *was still a great way off, his father saw him and*
> *had compassion, and ran and fell on his neck*
> *and kissed him.*
>
> —Luke 15:20

Often I have returned to the Lord after having spent time in unhealthy patterns and behaviors. I have squandered my estate, the good that could have been, and find myself settling for slop (Luke 15:14, 16).

I don't even like to think of the times that I have made the same mistakes and gone back to the old destructive patterns. This story in the Scriptures gives a vivid picture of God's acceptance every time I choose to return to him.

Even while I am a long way off, my Father sees me coming and has compassion for me. He runs and embraces me although I have hurt him and made a fool of myself. This doesn't sound like the picture of a disappointed father that I would expect.

All right, I've blown it again! I have done things that I really regret now, but my heavenly Father is waiting for me with open arms.

Father, remind me that you are waiting for me with an embrace, not a look of disgust.

BETSY'S POEM

I cannot recollect the past,
Or experience relationships lost;
Every sunrise and every sunset
Which went unseen, cannot be
    recalled.
Yet so much awaits me!
The beauty and simplicity of life
Are my most valued possessions,
And unity with your Son is my
    treasure.

Then our mouth was filled with laughter,
And our tongue with singing.

—Ps. 126:2

When I am at my worst, when things seem over-whelming, or when I feel low, I seek the comfort of my friends. God has provided me with loving, supportive people who lift me up when I can no longer stand alone.

It helps to share my tears, my frustrations, and my fears with others. I find that I am not alone; there are many who are hurting in the same way I am. Talking helps, but laughing gives my heart a lift.

It seems so simple, yet it works like a miracle! Laughter clears my thoughts and gives me the desire to continue. I'm thankful that God gave me the ability to laugh.

Sometimes I get so serious about life. True, there is lots of pain and sadness, but a person can only take so much sorrow! There are times in my life when I wondered if I'd ever be able to laugh again; the pain of the past coupled with the anxiety of the day caused me to feel hopeless. It was at those times that God gave me the gift of laughter.

It feels so good to let loose and laugh! It brings healing to my aching soul.

Lord, thank you for soothing my heart with laughter.

Behold, how good and how pleasant it is
For brethren to dwell together in unity!
—Ps. 133:1

Great, it's time to get out the Christmas decorations!" My husband and children are ecstatic, but I am less than enthusiastic. Getting ready for the holidays is overwhelming to me. The seasonal traditions involve lots of confusion, noise, and food in our family. I'm not sure my recovery is ready for this, but ready or not, here it comes!

When the reds and greens are placed next to my favorite blues and mauves, I begin to get a little agitated. Then comes the ordeal of decorating the tree. My sweet little children turn into maniacs when all the fragile ornaments appear. I try to bite my tongue and hope that the majority of my ornaments will withstand the pressure of little fingers.

As I begin to think about baking and buying presents, the anxiety level really rises. I am trying to remember what Christmas is really about so I don't get caught up in the compulsiveness of the season.

I am capable of making new choices this year! I choose not to become obsessive about the way the house looks, even if things are out of place. I will not endanger my recovery just to please others with my baking. Those cheerful little faces are much more meaningful than any of the breakables on the tree!

Father, help me dwell pleasantly with my family.

December 4 – EXCEEDING GREAT JOY

When they saw the star, they rejoiced with
exceedingly great joy.
                                                —Matt. 2:10

When I woke up this morning my kids were wild with excitement. They were looking out the window and talking about the beautiful sunrise. The sky, dotted with clouds, was a brilliant burst of pinks and purples. I was thrilled to be able to share that view with my children.

Joy has not been a big part of my life. For years I was so involved in keeping the secret of my eating disorder that I had little time to enjoy life. My heart was so full of pain that I doubt I could have enjoyed things even if I had taken the time to notice them.

Since I began my healing process I have had much pain. It has taken some time to peel back the layers of my heart that died many years ago. Even in the pain, though, I have become aware of new feelings stirring in me.

The sunrise this morning was yet another example of the changes that are taking place in my life. Things are not perfect, nor even close to being pain-free. Yet the new-found feelings of joy are popping up more and more often. I am grateful for the ability to rejoice over the little things in life!

Lord, I thank you for allowing me to live long enough to experience real joy!

He lovingly and devotedly examines his creation,
Which he skillfully molded in his likeness.
He carefully holds me in the palm of his hand,
And meditates on his plan for me.

He gives me freedom, and a will to make choices,
But he desires a close, loving relationship with me.
He sends a companion to dwell in my heart.
So I will never feel lonely or abandoned.

He sends his Son to die on the cross.
Because he wants me to know how much he
    loves me.

Tears run down his cheeks as I reject his gifts
And replace his will with things of the world.
Finally, broken, weeping, I accept Jesus as my Lord,
And ask the companion to dwell in my heart!

He patiently continues his work of melting and
    molding,
And in his hands I begin to take the form he
    intended.
With joy replacing fear, my head bowed, on bended
    knee,
I praise the Creator; I worship his holy name!

He wonders why it took so much pain and
    brokenness
Before I accepted his free gift of grace.

> *Your hands have made me and fashioned me.*
> —Ps. 119:73

Once upon a time there was a famous designer. He was the most sought-after designer in the whole world. Each item he made was a one-of-a-kind creation!

For ages this designer sketched and planned; he thoughtfully worked to create the most beautiful garment for me. He loved me so much that he went to great lengths to gather just the right materials needed to put together my attire.

The suit had to be just right; it was being fashioned to bring out the best of my inner and outer traits. The designer chose to weave the fabric himself, because he wanted to ensure that it was of the highest quality. He crafted all the accessories to bring out the beauty of the design. Carefully he cut the pattern for the costume.

He took his time as he worked, and lovingly stitched each seam. When he was finished he was pleased with his work; it was perfect in every way.

Now the garment is mine! If I imply that the design is not all that I expected, it is like rejecting the designer. Instead I choose to accept it with a thankful heart!

Father, help me accept your design gratefully.

*I love the LORD, because He has heard
My voice and my supplications.
Because He has inclined His ear to me,
Therefore I will call upon Him as long as I live.*
—Ps. 116:1

The Lord has been a faithful friend to me. No matter how far I wander from him, he never leaves me. God is there to listen to me when no one else has time. He does not get tired of hearing from me!

There was a time when I doubted his love for me. I grew up being afraid of God; I thought I had to be perfect to earn his love. When I was unable to attain perfection, I was sure I was unacceptable to God.

I grew so depressed that I tried to take my own life. When I did not succeed, I realized that I needed God's help. He heard me when I cried out to him, "Lord, help me!"

In the midst of my pain, he touched my heart and filled my emptiness. He used the love of friends to give me hope. I am so thankful that the Lord hears my voice!

My fear of him has turned to love. I no longer hide myself from God because of my imperfections; I know that he is willing to listen to me, no matter how unacceptable I feel.

Lord, thank you for hearing me when I talk to you.

*There is therefore now no condemnation to
those who are in Christ Jesus, who do not walk
according to the flesh, but according to the Spirit.*
—Rom. 8:1

I hated to purge, but I loved to purge. I hated to binge,
but I loved to binge. I hated my lack of control, but I
loved the control I gained when I did not have to eat. I
hated myself, and I felt condemned for my behavior.

This battle raged within me for many years. Each
time I hung my head over the toilet, I promised God
that I would stop abusing my body. I knew in my
heart that what I was doing was wrong, but I felt powerless to stop. I condemned myself each time I broke
my promise to God.

My body was at war with my heart. In my heart, I
longed to give up my eating disorder, but I lacked the
tools to cope with life in a healthy manner. I believed
that I had to be perfect in order to earn God's favor, but
I was anything but perfect. I felt hopeless, and I wanted
to die.

I cried out to God for help, and he did not fail me! I
have learned that the condemnation was all self-
imposed. In Christ I have been set free from the burden
of all my wrongs; he does not condemn me.

*Father, thank you for freeing me from condemnation and bathing me
in your love.*

*For by what a man is overcome, by this he is
enslaved.* —2 Peter 2:19b NAS

As I studied this verse with a friend, I was amazed by its application to my life. There are many invisible chains in my life; I am in bondage to obsessional thinking, material desires, confused priorities, perfectionism, and food.

When I begin my day overwhelmed by the fear of bingeing I become a slave, held in prison by food. Perfectionism limits my ability to relate to people; I am in bondage to my high expectations for others. No one could possibly live up to my standards! Obsessive thoughts hold me captive in a tiny cell.

I have found my freedom in Christ. He is breaking down the walls of my prison. God's Word says, "But God be thanked that though you were slaves of sin, yet you obeyed from the heart that form of doctrine to which you were delivered. And having been set free from sin, you became slaves of righteousness" (Rom. 6:17–18).

Father, free me from slavery to unhealthy things. I want to be overcome by your love.

> *Now no chastening seems to be joyful for the present, but painful; nevertheless, afterward it yields the peaceable fruit of righteousness to those who have been trained by it.*
>
> —Heb. 12:11

The word chastening brings to mind a form of punishment, but it also means preparation and training. It hurts a lot when God prunes my branches (John 15:2). I feel pain when part of me is being refined.

Although it is not pleasant, I can see how God uses the pain in my life to prepare me and train me. I am able to relate to those who struggle with eating disorders and with the memories of sexual abuse. Had it not been for my own pain, I would be unable to give support and encouragement to others.

The pain in my life has become my passport into the lives of those around me. God has been skillfully preparing me for the future through things that have brought me much sorrow. I have peace inside where there was none before.

I would love to have been born fully equipped for life. I'd rather not endure this pain, but I am beginning to understand the reasons for it.

Father, give me peace in the midst of the pain.

> *But the wisdom that is from above is first pure,*
> *then peaceable, gentle, willing to yield, full of*
> *mercy and good fruits, without partiality and*
> *without hypocrisy.*
> —James 3:17

At times it is difficult for me to distinguish whose voice I am listening to. The thoughts in my mind can come from many sources.

I know in my heart that it is Satan's desire to destroy me; he would love to see me consumed. The way he attacks is through my thoughts. I always know when he is speaking: I feel hurried into action; I have an overwhelming sense of guilt, or I feel confused and out of control.

God, on the other hand, speaks to me in a quiet voice. He gently leads me to change, and I am aware of specific areas that need attention. I know truth when he speaks. He does not cause me to feel confused or panicked. God convicts my heart but does not condemn me.

My eating disorder has been founded on lies and deceit. I want to make sure that what I'm hearing, and the direction I am taking, is based on truth.

Heavenly Father, teach me to know your voice. Help me to spend time listening, so I can receive your insight and wisdom.

For You, Lord, are good, and ready to forgive,
And abundant in mercy to all those who call
upon You.
—Ps. 86:5

I have found God to be faithful in forgiving my sins. In 1 John 1:9, I read, "If we confess our sins, He is faithful and just to forgive us our sins and to cleanse us from all unrighteousness." I have to take an active role in receiving God's forgiveness. My part is to confess to him.

Once I have received God's forgiveness for all my lies, deceit, anger, and hatred, I have a clean start. I have difficulty accepting God's forgiveness, because I know that in turn I have to forgive others.

I was not raised in a nurturing home, and I did not receive love and respect and acceptance. As a result, I find it hard to forgive others. God is slowly teaching me to forgive; I am not capable of truly forgiving without his power.

He has forgiven my sins, just as he promised, and he is providing me with the tools to forgive others as well.

Lord, make me aware of the sins I have not yet confessed to you.
Please give me your grace to extend forgiveness to others.

*This hope we have as an anchor of the soul, both
sure and steadfast, and which enters the Presence
behind the veil.*   —Heb. 6:19

I can remember, as a child, anticipating a special
Christmas gift. Now and then I hoped for a passing
grade or a part in the school play. I hoped that a special
person would reciprocate the feelings I had. Sometimes my hopes were rewarded; occasionally I got
even more than I hoped for.

As I have matured and my life has become more
complex, I have gotten rather cynical in my outlook on
life. I expect only what I have paid for with money,
service, or time. I try to remind myself that hope af-
fects the quality of my life.

When I hope for good results, I find myself doing my
best. When I am hopeful, I am more cheerful. Hope
keeps me from quitting; it can be the reason for success.

There have been times when I have felt hopeless.
My eating disorder seems like an overwhelming obsta-
cle some days. I find hope in the Lord; he is giving me
the power to overcome even the seemingly hopeless
things in my life.

*Father, help me to find my hope in you. Give me the courage to hope
for the best.*

> *And He said to me, "My grace is sufficient for*
> *you, for My strength is made perfect in weakness."*
> *Therefore most gladly I will rather boast in my*
> *infirmities, that the power of Christ may rest*
> *upon me.*
> —2 Cor. 12:9

Loneliness, fear, anger, pain—I cannot overcome these alone, because I am powerless! There is nothing within me that is capable of healing years of pain. I have tried everything to relieve myself of the shame and guilt that plague me.

Numbing myself with food and abusing my body with an eating disorder did not heal my broken heart. Restricting my food intake did not give me the control I desired; I only lost more control.

The healing of my deep emotional wounds is God's work. His ability to heal me takes over when I accept my inability to do it for myself! I can see his power in my powerlessness.

> *I do not have to feel lonely,*
> *My faithful God is always there.*
> *When fear overwhelms my being,*
> *God keeps me in his care.*
> *When I allow anger to lead me,*
> *Through surrender, I lay it aside.*
> *When the pain of life overtakes me,*
> *God dwells in me; to self I have died.*

Lord, remind me that I do not have to be sufficient to deal with my problems because you are!

*Therefore lay aside all filthiness and overflow
of wickedness, and receive with meekness the
implanted word, which is able to save your souls.*
                                    —James 1:21

I know a man who started smoking cigarettes when he was sixteen. Within a year he was smoking one pack a day, and he continued smoking until he was fifty-seven. By that time, he was consuming three to four packs of cigarettes each day.

At times he would try to quit smoking, but he never succeeded in kicking the habit. Suddenly his voice became raspy, and he went to see a doctor. The doctor said, "We will have to do a biopsy on your throat; you need to stop smoking."

As the man left the doctor's office, he gave his freshly opened pack to the receptionist; he has never smoked again in eleven years. The biopsy was positive, but the cancer was arrested with radiation. His many attempts to quit ended in failure until he was properly motivated.

What's the magic word that will motivate you to give up your addiction? What will it take to get serious about your health and your life? Eating disorders do not cause cancer, but they are hazardous to your health.

———————————

Father, give me the motivation to find the reason for my addictive behavior. I trust you to give me the strength to overcome my addictions.

And do not be conformed to this world, but be transformed by the renewing of your mind.
—Rom. 12:2

I have spent hours trying to perfect my appearance, believing that outer beauty would give me the sense of acceptance that I craved. I bought into the world's system of values. My eating disorder was an attempt to bring my looks into line with what was acceptable to others.

As I concentrated on the physical aspect of my body, my inner strength began to fade. I learned that God values me for different reasons than the world does. I am working on changing the beliefs I have; in this way I am renewing my mind.

"For man looks at the outward appearance, but the Lord looks at the heart" (1 Sam. 16:7b).

"Charm is deceitful and beauty is vain, but a woman who fears the Lord, she shall be praised" (Prov. 31:30).

"Do not let your beauty be that outward adorning of arranging the hair, of wearing gold, or of putting on fine apparel; but let it be the hidden person of the heart, with the incorruptible ornament of a gentle and quiet spirit, which is very precious in the sight of God" (1 Peter 3:3–4).

"For bodily exercise profits a little, but godliness is profitable for all things, having promise of the life that now is and of that which is to come" (1 Tim. 4:8).

Lord, help me believe what you say is true.

*But He said to them, "I have food to eat of which
you do not know."*
                                        —John 4:32

Sometimes I am afraid I will eat everything in sight.
At other times it is hard to make myself eat anything at
all. I have an eating disorder, and I struggle to balance
my eating habits.

Since I spent nine weeks in treatment for my eating
disorder, many of my obsessive habits with food have
diminished. I am not actively practicing the behaviors
that controlled my life for years, but I still tend to look
to food for comfort.

I thought that only eating-disordered individuals focus on food, but many of my friends who are "normal"
eaters also use food to distract them from life. Some of
my favorite television shows feature people doing not-
so-normal things with food.

People without eating disorders sometimes eat too
much, and at other times they don't take time out to
eat. I hear my friends discussing what they had for dinner the night before and drooling over what they plan
to eat for lunch.

I know people who seem to have a healthy self-
image but have trouble accepting part of their body.
Almost everyone deals with the things I face to some
degree or another. I'm not so strange after all!

Lord, give me the grace to accept myself.

> *For He stands at the right hand of the needy.*
> —Ps. 109:31 NAS

When I share the story of my struggle with bulimia, I often hear from others who are hurting and needy. Once after I had given my presentation a fifteen-year-old boy asked to speak to me.

He thought he was alone; he had heard of women who lived under the torment of anorexia and bulimia, but he did not know of any other males with those diseases. He needed to know he wasn't crazy or weird.

He had never told anyone his secret: each time he ate, he purged by taking fifty laxatives to rid himself of the food. Being sexually abused from the age of four had left him feeling dirty and ashamed. He hated his body.

By revealing his secrets he realized his need for help! Although he felt scared and almost hopeless, God provided him with a place to feel safe and start his recovery process.

Lord, be with those who are in need. Thank you for giving me the opportunity to progress in my recovery so I can give hope to others.

Hear my prayer, O LORD,
And let my cry come to you.
—Ps. 102:1

I was sexually abused for years. My abuser told me that he would kill my family if I ever told anyone the secret, so I kept the fear, the pain, and the abuse silent. Inside I wanted to die.

My eating disorder was a slow form of suicide. Bingeing, purging, and starving myself kept me numb. As long as I could stay focused on my body and food, I did not have to talk or remember. I was not self-destructive for no reason; there were many reasons for my self-hatred.

With the help of a caring therapist I have begun to work through some of the memories that I had hidden under my eating disorder. It has been a long, painful process, but I am no longer obsessed with food.

God heard my cry for help; he heard the prayer of my heart when I was too weak to utter it aloud. Why are you abusing your body? There are always many reasons. Seek him; he will bring you hope and help.

Father, help me as I continue to uncover the reasons I want to hurt my body. Hold my hand as I discover the truth.

> *For the battle is not yours, but God's.*
> —2 Chron. 20:15

What can I do to overcome the horror of pervasive, numbing, debilitating fear? Since I experienced traumas that caused me to be fearful, I have a hard time not allowing my fears to control me.

I have first-hand experience in emotional trauma, as well as physical abuse. My fears are not imagined; they are very real. My problem is that I let the fears from the past control my ability to live in the present.

Some of my fears overwhelm me to such an extent that I can become physically ill. I have learned to take care of myself by getting as much information as possible to allay my fears. In this early stage of my recovery, I have done all that I can to avoid situations that trigger my fears. I don't want to jeopardize my recovery.

Avoiding fearful circumstances is not always possible. I have found the courage to face many of my fears through my faith in the Lord. He is with me when I feel afraid; I don't have to fight this battle on my own.

Lord, give me the courage to be brave, the wisdom to avoid dangerous situations, and the knowledge to deal with them when necessary.

For unto us a Child is born,
Unto us a Son is given;
And the government will be upon His shoulder.
And His name will be called
Wonderful Counselor, Mighty God,
Everlasting Father, Prince of Peace.

—Isa. 9:6

As I walked on the beach one day, many thoughts rushed through my mind. I knew I needed to see a therapist, but which one? I wanted to choose the one that would be the very best!

As I attempted to determine who the best therapist would be, I became more and more confused. I had many to choose from. Each had individual techniques, views, and skills. I was not sure which therapist would be most helpful, and my thoughts continued to bounce from one choice to another.

Soon a beautiful thought entered my mind. Jesus is called the wonderful Counselor! Yes, my choice of an appropriate human therapist was important. But I was relieved to realize that whatever choice I made, Jesus Christ would always be my wonderful Counselor. Even in my predicament over which therapist to choose, I could ask for guidance from my heavenly Counselor! The choice no longer seemed overwhelming.

Lord, thank you for providing me with human advisors. Help me to learn to listen to your counsel.

*"If you then, being evil, know how to give good
gifts to your children, how much more will your
Father who is in heaven give good things to those
who ask Him!"*

—Matt. 7:11

I have a son who is eight years old and a daughter who
is five. At this time of year I love to shop in the big toy
stores for their Christmas gifts.

I spend hours looking at things I would like to buy
for them. It brings me great joy to know I am giving
something that will make them happy, and I am always
a little saddened because I cannot buy them everything they want.

I am awed when I think of how limited my ability to
love is, compared with God's infinite, unconditional
love. I know that my own selfish desires often get in
the way of loving my children; God does not have that
problem!

My heart breaks when my children make choices
that are not best for them. It is hard for me to stand by
as they make mistakes and learn lessons. If my heart is
torn, think how much more God grieves when I settle
for less than his best for me.

His gifts for me include a life full of challenges and
growth, but I have chosen to stay hidden behind an
eating disorder that retards my maturity. I am making
the choice to lay down my "toys" and accept what God
has to offer.

_____

*Father, help me believe that your gifts are better than what I have
settled for in life.*

*When Jesus saw him lying there, and knew that he
already had been in that condition a long time, He
said to him, "Do you want to be made well?"*
                                                —John 5:6

During the thirteen years that I was controlled by eating disorders, I made many attempts to "get my eating under control." Countless times I vowed to stop abusing my body, but I was never able to follow through with my promise.

I am convinced that I was never before ready to let go of my disease. It was comfortable, or at least familiar. I thought the patterns I had developed were working for me. I had no other tools with which to cope with life; I did not really want to get well.

After I had been in that condition for a long time, I became hopelessly depressed and extremely suicidal. I knew I could not go on living that way. The very thing that for so long had brought comfort and a sense of control to me was now in control of my life!

Suddenly my attitude changed. I had been clinging to my eating disorder desperately, and now I wanted to get away from it as quickly as possible. I truly wanted to be healthy and to live life without being controlled by food.

Do you really want to get well, or are you still comfortable being sick?

———————

*Lord, thank you for the desire for wholeness. I am grateful that I lived
long enough to get well.*

> *But Jesus turned around, and when He saw her He*
> *said, "Be of good cheer, daughter; your faith has*
> *made you well." And the woman was made well*
> *from that hour.*
> —Matt. 9:22

Trust does not come easily to me. Faith in people, in God, in just about anything is next to impossible because I was violated as a child. I grew up thinking that everyone was out to get me.

It was hard to accept what people said as truth because my trust had been abused so many times. How could I trust people, after those closest to me were abusive?

I lived my life trusting no one and having faith in nothing. Eventually I saw that my methods were failing. I was desperate and needed help. I had to trust someone or die.

I know now that God gave me the courage to reach out for help, or I never could have done it. He led me to Remuda Ranch, where I began the process of learning to trust. Before I entered treatment I told God, "I believe this is where you want me. Please keep me safe and make it work!" It was a minute-by-minute task to trust the staff, the doctors, the program, and even the cook. God took the minuscule particle of faith in me and used it to begin to heal me.

Father, thank you for planting the seed of faith in my wounded heart. Please continue to heal me from my inability to trust you and others.

*And she brought forth her firstborn Son, and
wrapped Him in swaddling clothes, and laid
Him in a manger, because there was no room
for them in the inn.*

—Luke 2:7

The Christmas story brings such hope to my heart!

The Son of God was not born with fanfare, and
many did not believe who he was. He made his arrival
in a stall filled with hay, and the audience consisted of
his earthly parents and the animals in the stable.

This is an example of how God can take seemingly
overwhelming circumstances and use them for good!
If the Son of God could make headlines in history with
his humble birth, I believe God can make something of
me, no matter what my background.

God doesn't use the world's methods to bring about
miracles! He does not require front-page coverage to
change lives. My name hasn't been up in lights or my
picture on magazine covers; nevertheless, the Creator
of the universe is making me new!

I am the product of a hurting family. My body has
been abused physically and sexually, and it was racked
by years of an eating disorder. Still, God is using me to
do good work for him! He is able to make something
beautiful of you, too, no matter how hurt you are inside.

Father, thank you for using me to do good work in spite of my past.

> *"Enter by the narrow gate; for wide is the gate and*
> *broad is the way that leads to destruction, and*
> *there are many who go in by it. Because narrow*
> *is the gate and difficult is the way which leads*
> *to life, and there are few who find it."*
> —Matt. 7:13–14

I was used to abusing my body; it almost felt comfortable. Eating disorders had been a part of my life for so long that I had come to accept it as normal. I resigned myself to the fact that I would live the rest of my life obsessed with food and my body. I thought I would continually worry about what others thought of me.

There are lots of ways for people to deal with the pain in their lives. Many choose to use drugs to numb their feelings; others obsess about sex. Alcohol is a socially acceptable way to escape pain; drinking is even a way to gain acceptance in some crowds.

Some people cling to a strict standard of religious ethics in order to find approval. Some of my friends shop compulsively; it's not illegal or fattening, so they think it's a healthy way of filling the emptiness. People do all sorts of things to find acceptance and love.

I want to be healthy; I do not want to use or abuse or busy myself in order to avoid my feelings. It's tough, but I am convinced that I'll be happier in the end!

Lord, give me the courage to do life without a "fix."

*And He took them up in His arms, laid His hands
on them, and blessed them.*   —Mark 10:16

For years I tried to block out all my painful memories.
I stuffed myself full of food and then threw it up and
started over again. I kept myself busy so that I would
not think about the events that left scars in my heart. I
avoided going to bed because I hated the stillness and
the quiet. It was too easy to remember.

All my compulsive behavior did not take away the
pain; my attempts to numb myself only prolonged the
agony. Eventually I had to face the devastation in my
heart. Now I have begun peeling back the layers of
pain that have accumulated over my lifetime. It is a
painful process, but one that is necessary to my life and
health.

When the pain gets too great, I picture myself crawling into my heavenly Father's lap. He is not like
earthly fathers; he is always available, and he listens
patiently and lovingly. I can see myself sitting there as
he gently wipes away the tears of a lifetime. He is my
greatest comfort!

Father, hold me close and take my pain away.

> *Create in me a clean heart, O God,*
> *And renew a steadfast spirit within me.*
> —Ps. 51:10

I told myself lies for years. I closed off my heart to others, in order to protect myself from being hurt. I don't want to live like that anymore!

I am trying to shed the "old me." I don't want to keep practicing my eating disorder or the unhealthy thought processes that went along with it. To avoid pain, I numbed myself with food, and then to relieve my guilt, I purged. Now I do not have to resort to those old habits; I have new ways of dealing with life!

Unfortunately, part of the old me keeps hanging on. I am afraid to trust people, and I also can't trust God. I am afraid to be hurt like I was before, and I fear that no one is worthy of my trust. It is scary to allow myself to be vulnerable with others and with God.

I want to be completely new. I want to give up all of the old stuff and start over. God is able to give me a fresh start; I am thankful for that.

Father, create newness in me. Give me the courage to keep making changes.

I'm hurting, Lord, and I'm really afraid. Do you know what I'm going through right now?

I feel all alone, like there's no one who cares. How do I know that you're there for me?

My fears threaten to take over; I feel like I'm about to drown. If I reach out, will you be there?

Father, this stuff was not in my plans; I'm still waiting for "happily ever after." How can I be sure you're with me?

It seemed easier when I went with the flow, when I was following the crowd. Will I ever be strong, God?

Lord, these changes are hard, and I'm afraid that I'll never really be different. Please give me hope.

My mind is full of doubts, and I'm not sure whose advice to take! Will you speak a little louder?

I'm committed to life; I'm doing what it takes. I hope the thoughts of dying go away soon.

Thank you for being with me on this path. Please stay close so I can feel your presence.

> *A time to keep silence,*
> *And a time to speak.*
> —Eccl. 3:7

Because of my feelings of inadequacy, I worry some-times that I talk too much in my support groups. I don't want to appear arrogant; not everything I think needs to be verbalized.

I am encouraged when others share that they have benefited from what I've disclosed. I feel worthwhile when I am able to help others. It gives meaning to my pain when I see that others gain hope from me.

It is good practice for me to be in groups. People view things differently, and I always learn from listen-ing to their perspective.

Part of working my recovery is making phone calls when I am struggling. That is difficult; it's much easier to call when things are going well. But as I become willing to make the calls, I progress in my healing. Having a friend listen while I talk helps me put things in perspective. I enjoy listening to others when they are in need of my ears, too. Sometimes people just need to talk!

Lord, help me know when to talk and when to listen.